The Truth Never Dies

About the publishers

Published by J.Bento Publishers

ISBN J.Bento Publishers 978-0957330269
Edition July 2012

The Truth Never Dies

Valter Dos Santos

J.Bento Publishers

This novel is dedicated to my beloved grandparents

Blessed are the merciful for they shall obtain mercy

(Mathew, 5; 7)

Chapter I

Gina woke up early in the morning, prepared breakfast and made sure the children were awake, dressed and ready for school before she could even think of doing anything else. Usually at that time in the morning her husband, Michael, would already be at work at the television news centre. They had met when they were covering the Sydney Olympic Games for different TV stations. At the time they were both in their mid-twenties and working hard to succeed in their careers. Gina and Michael started dating and in less than a year they were living together and Gina was pregnant. They got married not long after their first child, Harry, was born. Gina then had to change the focus of her life and slow down in her career while Michael would take any opportunity he could to work hard and succeed as a TV news presenter and the chief editor of one of the most important TV news companies in the country. Gina had given up work after their third child, Kit, was born.

That morning Gina felt a strange feeling, a feeling that she couldn't explain. Her heart was beating fast and she was not able to focus on anything. She felt a strong pressure around her chest and her head started to ache. After giving breakfast to her three children – Harry, Grace and Kit – she drove them to school as usual, and when back at home she opened the door to welcome Juliana, the housekeeper and babysitter. Her heart was still beating faster than usual, giving her a very unpleasant feeling. Her hands were shaking and the image of her husband's face was coming up in her thoughts. She tried to ring Michael on his mobile phone, but there was no answer. Michael had worked the previous night on the preparations for the day of the general election, a project that he had been involved in for months. Assuming that her husband was very busy, she did not want to bother him by calling his phone again.

He must be very busy, she thought, trying to keep herself calm. *It's better just to leave it. He will call me once he's got a chance.*

Her heart was still beating faster than usual and her hands got even colder. The house phone rang at that moment. Gina ran from the kitchen to the living room to answer the call. With her heart beating even faster, an even more intense pressure around her chest, she answered.

—Hello?

—Gina?

—Yes, it's me. Who is this?

—It's me, Paul.

Paul Edwards was Michael's cousin; they had been very close when they were growing up. Paul was also a journalist and worked with Michael at the television centre.

—I am sorry to give you the news over the phone, but Michael has suffered an accident. He is now at Charing Cross Hospital. Can you meet me there as soon as possible?

Gina sat on the sofa, speechless. She could not reply.

—Gina? Are you OK? Please talk to me!

Gina took a deep breath and replied.

—I am here, Paul. I am fine. I am on my way to the hospital. I will see you there shortly.

She hung up the phone before Paul could say anything else.

It had been at Charing Cross Hospital that Michael's mother, Harriet, had passed away after having complications during a heart operation. Gina had been very close to her and had been through the pain of losing her at that same hospital with Michael. A feeling of panic took over her mind. Anxious, she shouted for Juliana.

9

—What happened, Gina? asked Juliana, who looked visibly worried. You look pale. Are you feeling well?

—Paul has just called, saying that Michael is at the hospital. I don't know exactly what happened. I have to rush to the hospital.

—Are you sure you want to drive now? Your hands are shaking and you are out of breath. Don't you think it is better to wait a little bit, until you calm yourself down?

—I will be fine, Juliana. I need to see him right now. Please pick up the kids from school in case I am not back home by then. There's some change inside the tin on the kitchen top. Use it for the taxi. Keep your mobile with you, as I'll keep you posted.

What would I do without him? How could I raise our children on my own? Those were the first thoughts Gina had once she was in the car on her way to the hospital. Gina's mother had died when she was still a baby, leaving her father to raise her. Her childhood had been full of premature responsibilities and disappointments. Gina grew up unable to relax and play with dolls, like other children of the same age, as she had to look after the housework while her father was away working. Michael had been her first love. The fear of losing him took over her mind and tears ran down her face. Pictures of the good moments with Michael were popping up in her mind. Tears were running down her face whilst she was driving.

In less than twenty minutes she arrived at the hospital, and to her surprise she found that the hospital's entrance was already surrounded by a circus of reporters, TV crews and lots of photographers. When she got out of the car she could not even open her eyes due to the many flashes coming from the cameras. The noise and chatter emanating from the reporters was very loud and confusing, and amongst the whole circus she could hear from far away a male voice asking if it was true that her husband had died while on his way to the hospital.

—Why don't you shut up? Gina shouted back at the crowd of reporters.

In the middle of the confusion she was embraced by Paul, who took her inside the hospital.

—I am sorry about the reporters outside, Gina, said Paul while walking her to one side. The press has found out about Michael.

—How is he? What happened? asked Gina, who was very shaky and about to lose control.

—We don't know exactly how he is, yet, Gina. Michael fell down the stairs and it was a very bad fall. I was with him when it happened and I am still shocked. I didn't think it had caused such bad injuries, but when I tried to talk to him he wouldn't respond. I panicked and called the paramedics. He has been taken to Accident and Emergency and I am still waiting for news. I called you as soon as I arrived at the hospital.

Paul hadn't finished speaking when a doctor approached and interrupted him.

The doctor was removing the mask that covered his mouth so that he could speak.

—I believe you are Mrs Barker?

—Yes, I am.

—I am one of the doctors who are looking after your husband …

—How is he?

—Your husband suffered major injuries. His brain was badly affected and there was major internal bleeding.

The doctor paused briefly and then continued.

—I am very sorry to have to tell you, but he didn't make it.

—Nooo! Gina screamed and burst out crying. No! Not my

11

husband ... He can't leave.

Paul held Gina tight and asked the doctor to give them some time alone. Gina was crying desperately while embraced by Paul.

Two police officers approached them and told Paul he would have to go to the police station to give his statement and clarify some details.

Moments earlier in the hospital theatre ...

Michael felt a strange feeling as if he had butterflies in his stomach. He could see the doctors and nurses around him and he could feel a ticklish sensation around his head. He felt his body to be very light and tried to move.

—Sorry, doctors, but I need to be back at the TV station so that I can get ready to go live on air!

Suddenly Gina's image came to his mind. Oh my God! Gina must be very worried, he thought. I need to tell her that I am fine. I hope nobody has called her and told her I am at the hospital. I know she would start panicking.

He tried to get himself out of the hospital bed. Suddenly the room was filled with an immense bright light and from among all the doctors and nurses in the room a woman came towards him and stood with her arms outstretched. The woman smiled.

—Hello son, she said in a very soft tone of voice that sounded as low as a whisper to his ears. We are reunited again!

Michael couldn't understand what was happening. At that moment all the doctors and nurses started to rush around him with equipments. They were all over his body with their medical instruments, but Michael couldn't hear them anymore. The sound in the room faded away and slowly the images were becoming blurry until the point where all that he could see was the woman who was there right next to him.

—What's going on? shouted Michael feeling very anxious. Doctors, can you hear me?

—They can't hear you, Michael.

Michael sat down on the bed. The room was getting brighter and brighter. The woman held his hands.

—You passed away, she said. The bonds that linked your soul to your body have broken. You are now no longer attached to your corporeal body. I am going to take you back home now, son. Close your eyes and don't think about anything else. Keep your mind relaxed. I can guarantee that Gina and the kids are going to be fine. At this moment they are being assisted by their spiritual friends and they are going to be fine ... Close your eyes and trust me, you're safe.

The room turned even brighter as if in an explosion of light and a warm sensation took over his spirit. The bright light turned into a twist of colours and they both suddenly disappeared in the air, leaving behind the doctors and nurses. In a few moments they had both left the earth.

Chapter II

The Towers

One month later ...

Michael woke up feeling strange, as if he had overslept for hours. Confused, he sat up in the bed and took a look around the room. The room was very spacious and it was furnished with big and tall furniture made of solid pine wood. There were paintings of fields and pictures of flowers on the walls. The room had very high ceilings and white walls and it smelled of a mixture of lavender and jasmine. Feeling very confused he stood up and walked towards the door that was situated at the end of the room.

I have to get out of this hospital, he thought.

Michael walked towards the door and opened it.

I have to go back home and see Gina and the kids; they must be very worried by now.

When he left the room he found a long corridor covered with floral paintings similar to the ones inside the room. There were wooden doors lined up next to one another all along the corridor. The corridor seemed to have no end. He tried to open the doors one by one, but they were all locked. The more he tried to open the doors with no success, the more anxious and scared he became. Running down the corridor Michael shouted, asking for help. He knocked on different doors and after a while he went down on his knees, feeling exhausted. Losing his breath, he cried desperately.

—Harriet! exclaimed Mateo. Michael has woken up. He needs you, my dear.

—Mateo, answered Harriet, I am so concerned that Michael won't accept his new reality; he is still so attached to the earth and to Gina.

—Calm down, darling. You know that we have all at some point in our existence been through the same. The passage is not easy for most of us. Some of us bring the same wounds that we carried in our latest life experience, and once you return it takes time for the wounds to heal. He will be fine, my dear, he will somehow understand. Now go and help him, my love. I'll meet you two later.

Harriet closed her eyes and disappeared in the air, reappearing almost immediately in the long corridor where Michael was. She found him on his knees on the floor, crying desperately. Reaching out to him, Harriet went down on her knees and embraced him.

—Son, I am here with you. Don't feel scared.

—Mother? What's happening to me? Where am I?

—You have been asleep for a while. It happens with some of us when we return home. Your spirit is still tired from the previous journey on earth and you're now getting used to our home again. It's normal to find things confusing and to get scared. You're now in a resting house made especially for spirits to rest upon their return to home.

—So is it true? I am dead? said Michael while escaping from her arms.

—Don't say that, please, you are not dead! We never die, Michael. We evolve, and we become better spirits, but we never die. Our existence is infinite. We were not created to die but to evolve and progress to become pure spirits.

Michael began to cry even more, covering his face with his hands. He was feeling exactly as she said – scared and confused.

15

—For how long have I been asleep? asked Michael after composing himself.

—We don't calculate time here as they do on earth. Here we don't have to worry about things like time, because here we know that life is infinite. But if it makes you feel better to know, on earth it has been exactly thirty days since your passage.

Michael, feeling very emotional, held her tight and kissed her on the cheek.

—I missed you so much, mother.

Michael had stopped crying but still had lots of tears in his eyes.

—You look so different from how I used to know you, he said.

—I have returned to a different form of myself. I look now as I looked hundreds of years ago when I lived in a small village in the countryside of Italy. My name then was Veronica, and it was then that I met my soulmate Mateo, whom I have been with ever since. I have lived on earth a few times since that experience in Italy, and we incarnated a few times together. On the most recent experience I incarnated as your mother, Harriet. Our spirit can take the form and shape of our choice.

—Why don't I remember any of this? Why is it that all I can remember is Gina, my kids, and my job? For me right now you are not making any sense. Things have to make sense in my mind, and right now they don't.

—There's a reason why you can't remember things right now, Michael. Your return to the spiritual world is still too recent. With time you will recover your spiritual memory, and then all your past lives on earth and your spiritual experiences will come back to you. When that day comes, you will then be able to understand everything that has happened to you and your loved ones during this recent life experience. Time is the best healer and also the best teacher.

Embracing each other, Harriet and Michael left the corridor by disappearing in the air. They appeared in the same instant in a field covered by flowers and trees.

—Take a look, son. This is home.

Amused, Michael took a look around to appreciate the place he had just rediscovered. The air was fresh in a way he had never felt before. The sky was blue and it was bright too. There were birds and butterflies. In the centre of the field there was a massive and impressive building with high towers that looked very much like a medieval castle. The building was surrounded by tall trees with long and thick branches. The place was very bright as if sun rays were shining there, too, but with much more intensity. There were what seemed to be other groups of people, some sitting on the grass, others walking and talking. Some individuals were alone, as if meditating or praying, and many others were in groups doing different sorts of activities. Domestic animals like cats and dogs could also be seen. The place had a peaceful and joyful energy. Near the tall gate of the castle Mateo was waiting for them under a tree.

—Hi, Michael. Welcome back home, said Mateo, smiling.

—It's a pleasure to meet you, Mateo, replied Michael. I am sorry I can't remember who you are and that I have no recollections of this world.

—You don't have to be sorry. You will remember everything when the time is right.

—So is this heaven, then? asked Michael, still looking amused by the place.

Harriet and Mateo smiled at his innocent question. They sat on the grass and invited Michael to join them.

—Yes, son, Harriet explained. This is one of several spiritual colonies within the spiritual world. There are several different colonies and they all look very different. Here is where you were living before you reincarnated on earth for your most recent experience. This colony is called the Towers, and it was named after the castle towers.

—So the castle is a replica of medieval castles on earth? asked Michael.

—No, answered Mateo, who adopted a very didactic manner, albeit one that was as smooth and calm as Harriet. The castles that were built on earth, like all the other buildings, were actually built by spirits while living incarnated on the earth. Spirits wanted to construct on earth and other planets a life that was similar to the one back home here in the spiritual world. Once incarnated on earth the spirits over the times reproduced places and teachings learnt here. Every new technology learnt in the high levels of the spiritual world is transferred at some point to improve the earth and other planets.

—So what are the other colonies like?

—Very different from one another. Each colony reflects the level of purity of the spirits who inhabit it ... In most of the colonies we have schools, we have temples to pray and meditate, and we have recovery hospitals for spirits like you who have just returned from their experiences on earth and need to recover and need extra care. We also have houses of arts, habitation houses, lakes, fields, and lots of similar things that can also be found on earth. The more advanced and elevated the spirits are, the less physical substance they need in order to exist.

—So, do you mean that the earth isn't the only planet that is inhabited?

—Of course not. Imagine what a waste it would have been of God's energy if he had created the whole universe and only one of the smallest planets had had the privilege of being inhabited! What a vanity to think that one small globe is the only one to be inhabited by reasoning beings. There's life in every single space in the universe, and I can guarantee to you that every single planet in this infinite universe is inhabited with living beings all working towards the aims of God's providence.

—Are all the planets similar to earth, then?

—No, son. They are all very different from one another. They are all prepared to receive and serve their inhabiting beings according to their different organisations and degree of elevation. Different planets have different sources of energy and have different types of matter. There are more advanced planets that are home to elevated and purified spirits, and there are less advanced places which home spirits who are still very primitive.

—Do you mean that we have to incarnate several times, and that every time we incarnate we inhabit a different planet?

—We do incarnate several times. As many times as is needed in order to reach perfection. Spirits incarnate for two different reasons: either for the purpose of a mission or for expiation. In order to attain perfection, spirits have to undergo all the vicissitudes of corporeal existence. We are all created simple and ignorant, and the troubles and learning of the corporeal existences give us more instructions and guide us to our common goal: to purify our spirits so that we can reach perfection! The earth isn't one of the pure planets and it's actually very low on the purification ladder. Most of the spirits living there are still primitive and have a long way to go before they attain universal knowledge.

—Are all spirits incarnated on the earth primitive spirits?

—Oh no. There are many illuminated spirits incarnated on the earth and on many other planets with the purpose of sharing their knowledge with inferior spirits. Jesus was one big example of a pure spirit who inhabited earth. In fact, Jesus was the purest being who has ever lived on earth, and one of the purposes of his passage on earth was to share with the ones living there the knowledge of creation. Many other illuminated spirits inhabited and still inhabit earth with the same purpose: to share learning with spirits who are still searching; to share new technology, new ways of thinking and behaving, and in particular to show the fundamentals of divine knowledge; and to love and respect one another. There are other spirits who are so primitive that they are not even on the same evolutionary level as the earth, though they live there for reasons such as being given the opportunity to experience a more elevated planet in order to accelerate their evolutionary process, or having the opportunity to be with a familiar spirit who's on a more advanced evolutionary level and who can teach that inferior spirit and guide it towards evolution, which is what Harriet and I did on a few occasions. Some spirits who aren't amongst the incarnated like us can also visit earth and other planets in order to fulfil a mission or even visit dear friends who are incarnated and still facing the suffering of the corporeal existence in order to achieve their goals ...

Michael was very enthusiastic about that last sentence and interrupted Mateo.

—So do you mean that we can go back to earth and visit our family?

—We can all go to earth and other planets depending on the degree of our elevation and the reason. We do so for different reasons. We go for visits and to verify how our loved ones are doing during their experience on the earth and to give them vibrations of love and encouragement so they can continue strong and motivated in their corporeal existence. We also go to earth on special missions to heal or to

20

guide a lost spirit, and we go for other reasons, but always after it's been permitted by our superior mentors on behalf of God.

—I have good news for you, said Harriet, smiling. I know how anxious you are to find out how Gina and the kids are doing, so we might be just about to find out. Mateo and I will take you to see them.

When Michael heard Gina's name his eyes filled up with tears and he was then overcome by a sad feeling. The whole experience had been overwhelming, and he still couldn't get his head around everything that was happening to him.

—We need to warn you, explained Mateo in a calm tone of voice, that once we are on the earth you cannot bring any kind of negative energy with you. You need to focus on positive thoughts and be very careful not to engage in sad feelings, as our energy can positively or negatively affect those around us, and we could cause a lot of distress if that happens. You will be brought back here immediately if we think that your presence is being harmful to those we are visiting.

—Will they be able to see me or talk to me?

—I am afraid not, my son, answered Harriet with her hands on his shoulders. They are in a different dimension than us. My son, this first visit to earth will be very difficult for you, so please remember that you need to be strong and keep calm for the sake of the ones you love.

The three of them held hands and disappeared, leaving the Towers.

—Come on, kids, let me fasten your seat belts.

Gina was getting her kids ready in the back seat of the car.

—We are going to see the giraffes, the monkeys ...

—What about the lion, mummy? screamed Kit while pulling his

21

sister's hair.

—Yes, dear. The lion will be there too! Now stop pulling Grace's hair please!

After locking the back doors, Gina got in the front passenger seat and looked with relief towards Paul.

—I am so glad that you are here, Paul.

—It hasn't been easy for you, has it? replied Paul, who was in the driver's seat.

He held her hand very briefly before continuing.

—You know that Michael was my best friend and I'll do anything to help you and the kids.

—I cannot imagine what I would have done without you and my friend Isabel's help. You two have been two angels in my life.

Gina seemed to be very tired. She had dark circles around her eyes and her skin looked dull and pale. The kids were arguing in the back seat. Kit was crying out loud while Harry and Grace were pulling each other's hair. Gina had to intervene from time to time and seemed visibly stressed. At that point Paul held her hand for longer, as if he was trying to offer her some support.

They arrived at London Zoo after forty minutes in the car. Once the kids were out of the car they seemed uncontrollable. They were running to different places and causing Gina more distress. After a lot of running she managed to get hold of the youngest ones. Gradually Paul managed to get their attention and started to explain things about the different animals. He kept them all quiet for a while by doing funny faces when telling tales about the animals. When they saw the gorillas they all went very quiet, as if hypnotised.

—You can relax, Gina, said Paul. They are entertained by the gorillas now. You look tired. I can see that the kids and the housework are driving you to the edge of a nervous breakdown. You need to be careful – that's not good for you.

—Thanks, Paul. It has been a tough time. I am trying to balance the freelance work, home and the kids, plus the fact that I still miss Michael. I still haven't had some proper time with myself to grieve and get over what happened. Harry keeps on asking about his father and so do Grace and Kit, though Harry is the one who actually understands that his father isn't coming back home anymore.

Michael was by their side, accompanied by Harriet and Mateo. He shed a tear when he heard Gina mentioning his name and the sad time she was going through. He knew that Harry was the closest to him and the most similar, too. Harry was always telling everyone that when he grew up he would be a journalist like his father. Michael started to remember all the good times he'd had with his kids and wife.

—I can see how much Harry must be upset by my absence, said Michael to Harriet and Mateo with tears in his eyes.

At that point, when Michael started to cry and got really upset, Gina felt very vulnerable. Her eyes filled up with tears. Affected by Michael's vibrations, she could not hold the emotions and began to cry.

—Are you OK, Gina? asked Paul, holding her hands.

—I am missing him so much.

She could barely talk as she had been completely overcome with emotion.

Paul embraced her and comforted her, saying that he would be there for anything her and the kids needed and that she should not worry anymore.

When Paul hugged Gina, Michael's sorrow turned instantly to anger and he started to shout at Paul.

—Leave her! Leave my wife alone! You stay away from her! I

never trusted you and now I see why ...

Being able to sense the anger coming from his father, Harry looked to Paul with fury in his eyes and turned violent towards Paul, kicking him on his legs.

—Leave my mother alone! he shouted. Don't you dare hug my mother!

Harry's face went red and he carried on kicking Paul's legs.

—You are not my father, he screamed. Stay away from her!

At that point Kit and Grace, watching their brother's behaviour, started to cry.

—Stop kicking him, Harry, said Gina, trying to control the other two kids at the same time. That's not nice. You are upsetting Grace and Kit. Stop it.

Still feeling a strong anger, Harry screamed at the same time as his father screamed.

—I don't want you to hug her. Stay away from her!

In the meantime, Harriet and Mateo held on to Michael's arms, trying to control his temper and calm him down.

The more Michael shouted, the more Harry did, too, and the worse the situation became.

—Let's go back, said Mateo, still holding Michael's arm.

The three of them left.

It took Gina quite a while to calm down Grace and Kit, who were crying and screaming because of Harry's angry behaviour. Gina apologised to Paul and said that it would be better if they just went back home.

On the way home Gina couldn't stop apologising to Paul. Once they got back to Gina's house, she thanked him for the trip and apologised for the incident once again.

—Don't worry, Gina, it's understandable. They are still very fragile and they miss Michael so much. Perhaps I shouldn't have hugged you. I'd better go home now and get some work done.

Chapter III
Back at the Spiritual Colony

—I can't accept that! Paul will not get close to my family!

Michael was still very upset, shaking and talking to himself.

—You need to calm yourself down, son, said Harriet with maternal authority. It's not up to you to decide that. Gina has her own will and no one has the right to interfere with anyone's free will. Michael, your thoughts and feelings can affect those around you, especially at this moment when Gina and the kids are so vulnerable after your departure. At the moment you started to cry and began to feel upset, Gina and the kids could sense your negative vibrations and that caused them a lot of distress.

—So you mean that they knew we were there?

—No, they didn't know that we were there, but your bad energy was felt. Some people are so vulnerable that they can open themselves up to strange energies and that was the case then. Gina and your children, especially Harry, are feeling very vulnerable right now, which makes them easily influenced by any sort of negative energy, such as the one you just brought with you. Maybe if they'd been in a different moment of their life and engaged in happy and positive thoughts, no outside negative energy would have had an influence, as they would have been protected. Gina is now very down and engaging in pessimistic thoughts, which unfortunately attract to her surroundings more negativity and inferior spirits who are on the same negative vibration.

Feeling a bit embarrassed, Michael took a long breath and went quiet for a moment.

—You mentioned inferior spirits, he said eventually. Could they also visit the earth?

Mateo noticed that Michael was calming down, and held his hand.

—Yes, Mateo replied, not just 'elevated spirits' or pure spirits, as you prefer to call them, can visit the earth. There are plenty of non-instructed spirits who are still very primitive and choose to be attached to the material world even though they have disincarnated. The earth is one of the imperfect planets where most of those who are living there are spirits on a very low rung on the evolution ladder, and therefore the level of negative energy is very high compared to more advanced planets. Those spirits carry a very dark energy and are in a very low energy vibration, only attracting even more disgrace and misfortune for their existence. They are spirits who have refused to evolve and understand the real truth of our existence. They remain attached to the earth for reasons such as addiction to material things like toxic substances, vanity, wanting to avenge someone who is incarnated – whatever the reason, it always shows that such a spirit is choosing to delay its progression.

Mateo realised that Michael was very confused after all that new information. They stopped by a house that was surrounded by a garden. The house had white walls, a wooden door and windows with violet flowers on the window sills.

—Son, this is your home. This is the house you owned here at the Towers before. Even though you can't remember anything prior to your latest experience on earth, I am sure once inside you will feel comfortable, and being at home will help you to recover your spiritual memory.

27

Noticing that Michael was about to ask a question, Mateo gave him some words of reassurance.

—Give yourself time to digest all the new information. Everything in its own time, Michael. Time is a healer. Now go and rest.

Michael felt very curious and could not stop thinking about Gina and his kids. His question popped out of his mouth, even though deep down he already knew the answer.

—So when can I visit my family again?

—I remind you to trust God, Harriet replied, for now it's better that you rest and learn the lessons that will help you to grow and develop your spirit. It's time to think of yourself and no one else. By the way, Michael, I forgot to mention: there is someone in there who is very excited to see you. I am sure that will cheer you up.

Once he got inside the house he understood what Mateo had said about it feeling like home. Even though he could not remember being there before, he felt a very warm and pleasant energy from the moment he stepped in the house. The feeling he experienced was of softness and bliss, as though he was in the most relaxing place he had ever been.

There was a very fresh scent in the air. He explored every single space of that house, entering every room and analysing every detail. There were picture frames everywhere, though no pictures in them. It was like they had been taken away. The house was similar to a house on earth, though it was pretty much perfect in its details. The house was all painted in soft pastel colours.

There was a flower garden at the entrance and another huge green garden at the back. To his surprise, when he opened the door that led to the back garden a Labrador jumped up at him, excited and moving its tail to express its happiness.

—Oh my God! Rufus, is that you?

The dog barked loudly and went around Michael in circles, jumping to express his excitement.

Rufus had been Michael's dog when he was a kid. Rufus passed away when Michael was eighteen years old, when Rufus was very old for a dog. They were very close partners and Michael had missed him dearly when he died.

—I can't believe it's you! My dog!

Michael embraced him and leaned his head against Rufus's head and shed a tear.

—I missed you so much. It's so nice to see you again!

Michael played with Rufus in the garden for quite a while. Later, when he felt tired, he sat on the grass by one of the trees and fell asleep.

Chapter IV
Liverpool – 1822

—I can't marry him, father. You need to stop this arrangement!

—Don't you dare raise your voice to me, young lady. I will raise my hand to you and teach you to respect me if I need to!

Mr Williams punched the wooden table with his right hand. He threw a fork at his daughter.

—Felicity, he shouted, this man is our chance to make money again! He will be your husband and you have no choice in the matter.

The young lady with long dark hair and blue eyes begged him.

—He has very young children working at his factory, father, and everybody knows about the poor conditions they have to work in; I saw it with my own eyes. The conditions that those poor little children have to work and live in are dangerous and not human. They are treated like animals. I saw a little girl who must be five years old, at the most; she had the saddest eyes I have ever seen and it was as if she was asking me for mercy in silence. I couldn't live with a man like that; you know how I feel about this child labour ...

Before she could finish her sentence, her father stood up and grabbed her violently by her arms.

—I don't give a damn if the children at his factory are healthy or not. I don't give a damn if he hits those poor little devils or not! He is our salvation, Felicity; he is our way out of the misery we find ourselves in.

Still holding his daughter and looking firmly into her eyes, the old man shook her violently and sat her down on the chair by the table.

—Tomorrow Mr Worley will be here with his son Peter at seven o'clock, and his son will ask my permission to marry you. You will come down from your bedroom to the living area, and you will give Mr Worley and his son a smile and say how glad and honoured you are about the news.

The old man left the room. Felicity remained on her knees, crying, feeling hopeless.

At that point the room was filled with a light that brightened the whole room. Two men who were invisible to Felicity approached her and both put their hands above Felicity's head, and in silence they began to heal her spirit. Although Felicity could not see them or how bright the room had turned, she felt at that moment calmer.

—Please, Lord, she said, looking up. Be with me. Help me find a way out.

The following day arrived. Miranda, a black lady who was the only staff member to remain working for Mr Williams after he went bankrupt, started to clean the house very early to ensure all the housekeeping tasks were done by the time the Worleys arrived. She did a deep clean in the house, and looked after the garden and the cooking for the dinner party.

Miranda had always been very dedicated to Felicity's mother, and when she fell ill with cancer, Miranda promised her she would look after Felicity if the worst happened.

When Felicity's mother passed away, Mr Williams began to drink more than he used to and became addicted to betting. He lost all of his assets apart from the house they lived in. All the other servants tired of being verbally abused by Mr Williams and, unhappy about the lack of payment for their services, left him with his young daughter. Miranda was the only one to stay, although her decision had nothing to do with Mr Williams. She wanted to keep her promise and look after Felicity because she cared about the child as if she were her own. The financial situation had not improved, and the arranged marriage was for him a way out of misery.

The carriage arrived outside punctually at seven o'clock. Peter Worley, together with his father and mother, stepped out of the carriage and were greeted by Mr Williams. Peter's father, Mr John Worley, was a very famous and rich merchant in the region. Although he wouldn't talk about it, everybody knew that the most profitable part of his business was the result of the slave trade, and the reason why he would not mention the nature of his business was not because he wasn't proud of it, but because the slave trade had become illegal in the United Kingdom.

Their conversation in the living room was awkward and formal. The groom and his family seemed impatient, as if they wanted to get the business over with and leave the house. The groom soon asked to see his future fiancée. Mr Williams knew how reluctant his daughter was to marry this man, but he had no choice but to call her into the room.

Mr Williams asked Miranda to call Felicity, who was ready in her bedroom. Felicity walked down the long wooden stairs. She was wearing a bright yellow dress, her hair was curly and shiny, and her face was as pale as porcelain. Everybody in the room stood up to see the young lady enter the room and they all complimented her on how beautiful she looked. She was visibly uncomfortable and very shaky. Peter's eyes were focused on her. He knew of her rejection of him, which had only made him even more attracted to her. He spent months obsessed with her and dreaming about the day she would be his.

—You're right, my son, said John Worley, admiring her. She is beautiful and will make a good wife.

—Felicity, said her father. The young Mr Peter has just asked me for my permission to marry you. And I have told him and his parents how honoured we are with this proposal.

Felicity looked at Mr John Worley.

—May I ask you something, Mr Worley?

The man was too surprised to answer, and Felicity carried on before he could even open his mouth.

—Is it true that you, Mr Worley, still send ships to Africa to capture innocent humans who are sold in different countries?

Her question went down like a bomb in the room.

—You're an insane little girl if you think you can question me like this, Mr Worley replied. You must feel stupidly very proud of your decadent father to dare and confront me like this. Do you think my son and I don't know that this marriage is your and your father's last hope in life? This is the only way for him to get some money and save himself from complete misery. You must be insane to throw your only shot in life away with such accusations.

—I don't love your son and he knows it. He has been after me for months and I have made my thoughts clear. I don't understand what makes him insist.

Mr Williams, desperately trying to find a solution for the mess created by his daughter, begged the Worley family not to leave. He threw himself at Peter's feet.

—Please, please don't leave. She will obey you as her husband and she will be a good wife. She will learn to love you, I am sure. You can teach her.

—We are leaving, said John Worley, heading to the door.

—Father, wait! said Peter. I like her. I have liked her since I first saw her. Let me marry her! Mr Williams is right; I will make her love me.

His father sighed and agreed to negotiate with Mr Williams, on the condition that Felicity was sent to her room out of his sight. Once Felicity had left the room, they all went to the dinner table where

34

Miranda was waiting to serve the dinner. Mr Williams and Mr Worley negotiated the wedding. Felicity's life was negotiated there at the dinner table as if they were all negotiating the life of one of Mr Worley's captured slaves.

Later that evening, after the Worley family had left the house, Mr Williams, drunk, went to Felicity's room and got hold of her. He threw her on the floor.

—This is to teach you a lesson: to never disrespect your man ever again!

He spat in Felicity's face.

Felicity stayed on the floor, crying. Miranda went in and sat down next to her. She rested Felicity's head on her lap. Stroking Felicity's hair, she sang a prayer in an African dialect.

Not far from the Worleys' house, there was an orphanage that was run by a woman and her son. The woman lived off the fortune left by her husband after his death. The man died five years after their wedding, leaving his wife Beatrice and his son Jonathan. Beatrice never surrendered to the wealthy lifestyle that her fortune could have brought her and her son, and since the early days of her marriage she dedicated herself to looking after her house and her son. She always found time to learn different languages and to learn arts. When her husband passed away, Beatrice went against all the traditional values of those times and began to dedicate herself to helping poor people. With the money left by her husband, Beatrice decided to convert her manor house into an orphanage and help the poor children who lived in the region. The house was enormous and could easily accommodate the children and continue to be a home for herself and her son at the same time.

With the Industrial Revolution there were lots of children executing hard work in factories around the United Kingdom and Europe. Liverpool, being one of the richest cities in Europe at that time, had a large number of children suffering from alcoholism and illness due to the poor living conditions. It was common to see children as young as four and five working in factories for long hours, six days per week, and sometimes not even being paid for their services. At that time many children were found abandoned by their poor parents and some ended up being left in the streets.

Beatrice raised her son Jonathan with the best education and he became a tall, handsome man, with similar principles and values as his mother. Jonathan had just graduated in medicine from the University of Cambridge. When he returned to Liverpool after finishing his studies, he committed to helping his mother with the orphanage. They both led a charitable life helping the poor children in the region. Jonathan was very dedicated to his mother, and he participated in every step of the orphanage project as well as doing his own work as a doctor at the local hospital.

—Good morning, son! said Beatrice.

Jonathan had just joined her at the table for breakfast. An old lady in a uniform was serving the food.

—Morning, mother. You look flawless today, as usual! Good morning, Ophelia – how are you doing today?

The old lady, who was one of several servants in the house, smiled at him and replied, saying that she was doing well, and thanked him for asking. She served his breakfast and went back to the kitchen.

Beatrice was reading the newspaper, and one story in particular caught her attention.

—Jonathan, listen to this: 'Ten children died yesterday at

36

Morley's Textile Factory. The children were found with severe symptoms of malnutrition and signs of violent treatment.' I am disgusted. Someone has to stop that man.

She passed the newspaper to her son, who carried on reading.

—'Ten children died yesterday at Morley's Textile Factory after working over sixteen hours per day, seven days per week. The children had bruises all over their bodies, which probably indicates bad treatment by the company ...'

Jonathan dropped the papers on the table in anger.

—Working for over sixteen hours a day? he said. I feel so angry! Everybody knows about the atrocities against children in that factory, yet nothing is done to stop them.

—I know, son. I feel the same, though unfortunately this is the cruel reality of our society. They have the money and power. Nobody seems to care for the children and in the end they are all treated as white slaves. What hurts the most is knowing that this is happening here just under our nose and there is nothing that we can do!

—One day I will find a way to stop all of this. Mark my words, mother, I will!

Beatrice and Jonathan's conversation started to fade away and the picture became blurred.

Chapter V
At the Temple

Suddenly Michael felt a warm feeling. He could hear birds singing. Opening his eyes, he realised that he had been asleep. He stood up feeling very happy. His astral memory was coming back to him. Rufus was there, excited, jumping on him. He picked Rufus up and received a lick from the dog, who seemed very happy to be with him.

Mateo and Harriet knocked on Michael's door moments after he woke up. He greeted them with a wide smile and hugged them both.

—I had a dream last night, and I think the dream was about my past life ... I mean, our past life experience.

Harriet and Mateo smiled and congratulated him.

—What about your surprise? Harriet asked, looking at Rufus. Are you happy?

—Yes, I am, said Michael whilst stroking the dog's head. But ... erm ... How ...? So animals are spirits too?

—The animals have a soul and their soul life is also infinite, explained Mateo. They continue to evolve as we do. Different from man, the soul of the animal does not have its own faculty and self-consciousness, which is the principal attribute of the spirit. The animal's soul is far from being similar to men's souls, and men's souls are far from being similar to God. For the animals, the men are God.

—You can tell us about your memory now while we walk down to the temple, said Harriet.

They walked slowly towards the temple and Harriet and Mateo

paid close attention while Michael told them the details of his dream. They walked along a road where beautiful large houses were located. Michael had told them about his entire dream by the time they reached the temple. Once they had arrived, Harriet and Mateo introduced him to some friends and entered the temple.

The temple had shiny marble floors that reflected the chandeliers on the ceiling. In the centre of the entry hall there was a three-level water fountain constructed from the same marble as the floor. There were groups of people all over the massive room and they all stopped when the picture of the Towers' minister appeared at the centre of the room in what appeared to Michael to be a hologram.

—In here, said Harriet, is where most of the colony's administration work is done. Inside the temple we also have the minister's office, the senate, and some other offices for some of the superior spirits who administrate our colony.

The minister greeted everyone and then began to deliver the message of the day.

—*Good morning to all my dear friends and residents of the Towers. The message of the day is about freedom, about free will. As you all know, we are all given the free will to take control of our own actions and to decide our own destiny. It's completely up to us as individuals to make the right decisions and choose to follow the right path. The right path is always the one that leads us towards God. When deciding our actions we need to consider if that particular decision is going to affect our spirit positively and help us to evolve and have a positive impact on the lives of those around us. If the answer is yes, and that decision will bring only benefits without bringing any harm or suffering, then that's the right path to be followed. Where love exists is where God lives. Also remember that for every act, for every decision taken, there's a*

consequence. Don't ever forget that we do not have the right to interfere directly or indirectly in anyone else's free will. We do not have the right to impose ourselves on any other individual without their consent ... True love respects the freedom and the free will of the other individual. All of those who try to enforce some kind of feeling upon someone else will live a life of lies, because the true love is a powerful feeling that requires freedom. To try and imprison someone is to end up by imprisoning ourselves with our own obsessions. We cannot own someone, but should walk side by side with them, always preserving the true meaning of our existence, which is the individuality of the spirit.
I would like as per usual to invite you all to pray with me. God almighty, the all powerful, bless us with your divine knowledge on another day. May we find the inspiration and knowledge needed to continue to move our spirits forwards towards purification ... I wish you all a blissful day. Go in peace, spirits of light.

Once the picture with the face of the minister had vanished into the air, people began to leave the temple.

—It seems like the message has touched you, Michael, said Mateo, noticing Michael's pensive expression.

—Yes, indeed. It had a lot to do with my dream last night, especially regarding people interfering in other people's free will. That girl in my dream had all her free will taken away from her.

Michael looked around the room before continuing.

—I am so amazed about all this new life that I didn't know exists. Why do we not carry the memory of what happened in our past? It's not fair!

—You knew this life existed, Harriet explained. And don't judge a divine law that you don't know. Imagine our past lives as being covered with a veil once we incarnate. This is a chance for every spirit to start

40

again. A chance to redeem a bad action, a chance to prove it has learnt the lesson, a chance to put into practice everything learnt throughout previous experiences without the influence of the past. The incarnation process works to purify our spirit. Imagine for example a spirit which, in its previous life experience, had committed a murder. How could that spirit obtain any benefit from reincarnating again if it was to be born with the full knowledge of the crimes it committed in the past? By having his spiritual memory covered up temporarily, that spirit can have a fresh and new start without carrying the weight of its past mistakes.

Harriet took Michael's hands in her own and continued.

—You are slowly recovering your spiritual memory. Last night you had a glimpse of some very important facts. Digest the information you received, think about each of those people, their behaviour ... appreciate what you have been given. The veil is still over your past for a reason, and the reason could be to trust God. Believe He is a father and He looks after all his children.

—Come on, Michael, said Mateo, tapping him on the shoulder. Let's live in the present. Ask me something with regard to what you have just experienced. The present, the only moment that really matters for all of us.

That helped to put a smile on Michael's face.

—OK. Let me ask you, how come you have a minister? Are there politicians here too?

—There are no politics here as on earth, Mateo explained. In the Towers we have superiors, which are very elevated and pure spirits that help with the organisation of our colony. It's always the most instructed and knowledgeable who instruct and guide their less instructed friends, remember? Our minister and senators are pure spirits whose mission is to share with us some of the knowledge we still haven't obtained yet, in the same way that I work in the dark zones near the earth, trying to rescue other spirits which are still inferior. In the universe it's all about progress, and we cannot progress if we don't share what we've learnt with those inferior to us. Every colony has superior spirits to those who inhabit it so they can benefit from thoughts and knowledge they are not prepared and not instructed for. We also have rules. We don't have to follow rules because we would be punished if we didn't; we follow rules because they bring us harmony, and we are all here striving towards the same goal. Here, for example, Richard Moore is the head of the ministerial department, and he is a very elevated spirit who contributes a lot to our community. He makes sure all the different departments are organised and that all the jobs and tasks are properly done. He is also our main contact with the high-level colonies. He is a very elevated spirit, as I said, and has chosen to guide us, who still have so much to learn.

—On earth, replied Michael, some people think that when we die we go to heaven to live an easy and lazy life beside angels and Jesus Christ. As I can see, this doesn't really happen here.

Harriet suggested they left the temple and walked towards the field so they could carry on talking. The three of them left the temple and walked along the long garden that decorated the front of the temple.

—Jesus is one of the purest spirits and the one closest to God, said Mateo. We all aim to learn and elevate ourselves to the same level of purity of soul as him. We are so far from his level of elevation that for now it is impossible for us at this stage to reach out for Him, which doesn't mean that He cannot reach us.

Mateo pointed at a bench near the entrance to the garden, and they all sat down before he continued.

—The rules and the work are always necessary, they dignify us.

We cannot just live a lazy life, as most people on earth think we can once we have left our material bodies. Imagine what a waste for the universe if everyone decided to stop and do nothing. We need to produce; we need to contribute to the universe. Each individual has to serve a purpose. Everyone has to fulfil a reason for their existence. The universe is constantly moving and we are part of it. Imagine the universe as an immense and vast society that needs everyone collaborating in order to keep the harmony. We need the nurses, the teachers, the rural men planting and providing the food; the workforces in the factories here are the same as they are across the entire universe. Spirits are always working to serve God and make his will happen. We have to always make ourselves productive. Here we have people working in the education area, teaching spirits in colonies where our fellow spirits are not as evolved as we are; we have guardians that guard our gates and also help on the lower level of the earth where non-educated spirits and spirits with dark thoughts insist on remaining. We also have builders that build our houses, artists, gardeners, and many other different types of job, just as any society requires. Work is valued here and on the earth, and it's through hard work that we are able to contribute to the universe. In the many other colonies, there are some which are much more intellectually superior to ours, and those are the places we are going to go once we have reached another level in our evolution – and of course there are places inhabited by spirits who are still very inferior and who are reluctant to obtain more knowledge and insist on keeping themselves blind to the truth. These places needs constant protection and visits. For example, I work at a hospital near the earth in a very dark zone where many spirits live in war. The sphere in which I work is a place where materialism is very dense and the beings there are still very attached to emotional traps such as envy, jealousy, strong passions and extreme sexual behaviour. I pay daily visits to the hospital our colony has built there, and along with other missionaries I work on the rescue of spirits who have decided to surrender and be taken to a colony of recovery. This is my way to help and serve God at this stage of my existence. I don't have to incarnate on inferior places any longer, and this mission is now something that helps me to evolve and enrich my spirit towards divine purification.

Mateo stood up and excused himself, saying that it was his time to go to work and help his companions at the hospital.

Harriet and Michael said goodbye to him. After he had left they kept in silence for a moment as Michael seemed to reflect on everything that he had just learnt.

—So, mother, said Michael. About what I told you before – my dream. It's so difficult to imagine that I was there and that I lived in that time.

—Yes, I know. We all lived together in that same time in Liverpool. And believe me we all had many, many other life experiences. We were all created completely ignorant.

—There were so many things happening. Felicity being forced to marry and so much suffering. I felt a negative energy that I have never felt before. I still don't know from all I have seen whom I was and what happened?

—All I can say for now is that we were all there. You, me, Paul and Gina ... We are still dealing with the consequences of the actions from that time.

After a whole afternoon together, Michael went back home where Rufus was waiting, happy for his arrival.

In a cafe in London ...

Gina had decided to accept one of the various invites from her best friend Isabel and meet up for lunch followed by a coffee. Gina and Isabel had met at university and had remained best friends since then.

—You need to get yourself together, Gina. It's been months since Michael passed away. You hardly leave home and hardly ever have time without the kids.

—I am fine, don't worry. I am getting my life back little by little. The kids are fine too. Harry still misses his father badly, but Kit and Grace are doing better. I also have Paul coming over almost every weekend to help with the kids. Since Michael died I have been trying to balance work with the kids, and they will always be a priority for me. But you're right; I need to start to look after myself a little bit more.

—And what about Paul? It's clear that he likes you. Have you been on a date?

—Stop that and don't be silly! He is only trying to help. He is being a good friend, that's all. He is a very handsome man, though, and even though ...

Gina paused for a moment, suddenly embarrassed.

—No, it's wrong for me to even think of another man. Anyway ...

—No, it's not, insisted Isabel. You're alive, don't forget! It's been almost a year since Michael passed away, and you need to get your life back. What a waste for your life to be there, stuck in that moment. It's time for you to get yours back. You still have so much to live for and experience. Paul is lovely, handsome, and your kids adore him.

—Let's change the subject, shall we? It's not often that I go out with you without the kids for a girls' afternoon, so let's have a bit of girls' time and talk some nonsense conversation for a while. No deep conversations for now, please.

—OK. But I insist Paul is a catch, and he is totally in love with you
...

They both laughed and changed the subject. Isabel drove Gina
back home and decided to stop by to say hi to the kids. Juliana was
sitting on the floor playing with the kids when the two arrived. When the
kids saw their mother coming home with Isabel, they all stood up and
ran towards them, giving them hugs and speaking loudly. The kids liked
Isabel very much and always enjoyed their time when she was around.
The kids asked Isabel to draw pictures with them and so she did. She sat
on the floor with them and started to play. Juliana took the opportunity
to say goodbye and left to enjoy her night off before the children could
notice her absence.

When Juliana was leaving, she bumped into Paul, who had just
arrived to pay a visit. When he entered the house he remained quiet for
a while, observing Gina playing with the kids. Once he was noticed, he
smiled.

—Hi everyone, he said. I took the afternoon off work, so I
thought I would stop by and say hello to you and the kids and check that
you are alright. I've also brought some sweets for the kids and chocolate
for their mother.

Gina blushed whilst Isabel and Juliana looked at each other and smiled.
Isabel took the opportunity to offer to take Juliana home. They all said
their goodbyes leaving Paul alone with Gina and the kids.

Chapter VI
Michael's Despair

Liverpool – The wedding

Alone in her dressing room, Felicity cried while doing her hair. She was wearing a long white dress and looked stunning, even though she was shedding tears of sadness. Outside her dressing room was her father, who was knocking on the door and asking her to hurry up, as the guests were getting impatient. She knew she couldn't escape; she knew that she had no option but to face it.

Felicity dried her tears and stood up. She took a long breath, as if trying to get herself some strength, and finally opened the door for her father.

—I am ready, she said.

Before they went down the stairs to head to the church, her father gave her a golden necklace.

—This necklace belonged to your mother, he said. Before that it belonged to your grandmother, and now it is yours. It is yours to carry with you and bring you luck. I know you're not happy with this, but one day you will realise this was the best thing that could have happened to us. You are a woman, and my best advice is to do what you are meant to do and obey your husband from now on.

—I said I am ready, said Felicity abruptly. Let's get this over with.

Walking down the aisle holding hands with her father, she looked stunning, with shining dark hair and deep, clear blue eyes.

The ceremony was very traditional and it went quickly. While the groom seemed to be very happy, Felicity remained the whole time with a very sad face. At the party after the wedding ceremony there was lots of music and there was also a lot of food and alcohol. Peter Worley proudly introduced his new wife to everyone. The just-married couple danced together and also joined the different guests' tables to thank everyone for their presence. Felicity was a stunning lady and enchanted everyone with her elegant manner. She knew that from that moment onwards her life had changed and she would have to obey her husband, which was what she had been taught her whole life: to serve her man. She engaged in conversations with all the guests, and appeared to everyone in the room to be the perfect wife.

On one side of the room, Peter's father was observing Felicity interacting and socialising with the guests. He called his son aside.

—She looks so gorgeous and gracious, John said to his son. Look around and see how people like her. They are all admiring her. Well done, my son. You just made an excellent acquisition.

The guests left, and Felicity's father got himself so drunk and out of control that he had to be taken away from the place. The groom's parents congratulated Felicity and said goodbye, leaving the new couple alone in the room.

—Don't feel scared of me, said Peter. We are now husband and wife.

Felicity would not look into his eyes.

—I have loved you since the first day I met you, and I am crazy about you. This is the happiest day of my life, Felicity. I know that you hate the fact that our marriage has been arranged by my family and your father, but I want you to know that I have chosen you, I always wanted you, and I wouldn't have chosen any other lady but you. I don't care that your father is a broken and drunken man. I've chosen you to be my wife!

—As you said, you have chosen me and you negotiated our

marriage. All I can say to you is that I know my place. I will obey you and be a good wife, as our contract says, but don't expect me to love you. Now, my husband, excuse me, because I am tired and I want to go to sleep. I'll see you in the morning.

Peter pulled her by her hair as she went to leave the room and adopted an aggressive tone.

—Don't make me turn nasty towards you, my wife. Tonight is our first night together as man and woman and you will do your duties as a wife.

—I am sorry but I am tired and I want to go to sleep. I am not ready yet for this. Please respect my wish.

Pulling her hair even harder, he dragged her through the room and up the stairs until they reached the bedroom. He then threw her on the bed and violated her. She cried throughout the whole act.

The picture faded away and Michael woke up feeling very tormented by the dream he'd had.

Harriet had invited him to spend the day with her; they had planned to visit the school where she worked as a teacher. She promptly arrived and found him waiting for her at the front door.

—Morning, son. Mateo was called to help a friend of his, Regina, with one of her missions. He did send his love to you though. Are you ready to visit the school? You look a little different. Are you OK?

—I have many questions troubling my mind after the dream I had last night.

—The school I teach at is not far from here. Perhaps we can talk while we walk? Go on and tell me what you remembered ...

—I had another dream about Felicity. This time she was getting married to that guy named Peter – Peter Worley. The vision was very sad, as she was forced to marry him and he ended up by ...

50

Michael could not finish his sentence and was visibly troubled by what he had just recalled.

Harriet continued his thoughts.

—Yes, I know what happened to her that night. That was a very difficult lesson for Felicity, though please don't forget that if that happened in her life, it was because she had pre-chosen before she incarnated to go through that experience.

—You mean that she chose to be sold by her father and to get engaged to such an evil man?

—No, she didn't choose that. Most of us before we incarnate for a new life experience can choose our family and choose the place that we are going to be living within. We can choose most of the challenges and obstacles we are going to face in order to make the new experience worth it, of course, always aiming to develop our souls by overcoming our weakness and going through tests. For example, someone who had experienced a wealthy life with power over others previously and made bad use of their richness and power by, let's say, abusing their authority or by humiliating other people, may choose – in order to improve such weakness – to incarnate again under difficult circumstances, such as poverty, so they can feel what previously they had made others feel. On the other hand, a spirit that has been proven to be charitable and to live a humble life whilst living a poor and modest life may choose to reincarnate and experience a wealthy life with the aim of resisting all the temptations money and power can bring. God always gives us the option to choose our path so we can learn from the new experience. Of course, a spirit cannot choose a wealthy life just for the luxury of it, but always because this will be beneficial to its development. Every trouble and obstacle in our lives is for our own benefit, as it should always be used to accelerate our learning process. One should never see a difficult situation that someone might be going through with pitiful eyes, but with the certainty that that difficult time is nothing more than a lesson so that that being can progress.

—Why would any spirit choose suffering?

—What is suffering for your material mind is actually a way to learn values. God, fair as He is, lets each one of us choose our way, and if we fail our mission, He always gives us a chance to make a new start, as any good father does.

—Back to the dream, or memory ... I still can't see me there. Was I there?

—Yes, you were there too. You were part of that same history and that wasn't the first time you all met. Your connection comes from a long time before. Again, I can't give you more information about what happened after that moment after the wedding, because as I told you before, the truth will come at the right time.

Harriet noticed that Michael had become distant and sad, and she embraced him.

—Always remember, she continued, that we all have free will and therefore we all choose our own path. God isn't unfair with anyone, son. If something happens, bad or good, it's because it had to be that way. We all, somehow, benefited from that experience.

—And what about Felicity? What happened in her previous lives that provoked all that suffering?

—Previously she had been obsessed with material traps such as wealth and power. In order to obtain status and wealth, she engaged in slavery deals and even prostitution.

—Was she also a slave merchant?

—Not exactly. She enslaved men who were in love with her. She used her seductive attributes to obtain wealth and power. She betrayed and cheated every single person who demonstrated any sort of good feelings towards her. In the name of power she killed many men. Once back in the spiritual world, she refused to see the truth, and for a long time she continued living on the earth, tormenting incarnated spirits. While living in the dark zones attached to the earth, she met Peter again – a spirit who had been obsessed by her beauty for many years. They began to feed each other and engaged in a very bad cycle of obsession, jealousy and destruction. They lived for many years lost in that destructive cycle. Mateo and I tried to reach her for many years, but only after much suffering did she finally accept our invitation to go to a recovery colony and learn more about spirituality. It was later at the Towers that she met Jonathan for the first time, and when she finally understood true love she then regretted all the suffering she had inflicted on others. Felicity and Jonathan fell in love, and knowing that Felicity had still to learn so much in order to elevate herself to the same level as him, Jonathan – who was more morally elevated than her – offered to reincarnate with her in order to help Felicity's spirit to progress. After studying her past mistakes, she had the courage to incarnate again. Peter at that time was on a completely different vibration. He was blinded by a very deep obsession for her. He was forced by superior spirits to reincarnate. We all went back to earth in order to help each other to progress to a new experience. And this was when we all incarnated in Liverpool in the nineteenth century.

—Can you tell me more? How did that experience in Liverpool end? What happened to Felicity? Did she marry?

—You will soon find out, Michael.

Michael was speechless, listening to everything as if a movie was going through his mind.

Harriet took a deep breath and continued.

53

—There's more to the present happenings linked to our past, though. Slowly you will remember and then be able to understand everything. We've got to have a balance, and even though we learn from the past, it's the present that should be taken as a gift from God, as a new chance to start again and make it right.

After walking amongst buildings at the centre of the Towers, they stopped at the front of a building that looked pretty much like a manor house.

—We've arrived, said Harriet. This is the school where I spend some of my time teaching. Let's go in.

Harriet showed him around and introduced him to a few of her colleagues. She explained some of the work they did in the school, such as teaching inferior spirits who were willing to give up their vices and follow a different path. The lessons given at the school were on basic knowledge about spirituality and the spiritual world. Each individual had to attend group classes and individual classes. In the latter each individual had to look back into their past and analyse each moment, trying to figure out what they could have done differently. At all times during the visit Michael's mind was focused on Gina.

Chapter VII
The Bank Holiday

Gina had decided to accept Paul's invitation after he insisted many times. She liked him not as a man but as a friend, and she appreciated all the attention and care he had given her since Michael had passed away. Her friend Isabel had offered to look after the kids while she was away with Paul. Gina didn't know where she was going; all she knew was that she was supposed to meet him at the airport and bring her passport with her. At the arranged time a car arrived: it was a driver who had been sent to pick her up and drive her to Heathrow Airport. It was very early in the morning and Gina didn't want to wake the kids. Juliana the babysitter was awake and she had made breakfast for Gina. They had become friends, and that morning while having breakfast together they shared Gina's excitement about going away for the Easter bank holiday weekend with Paul.

After saying goodbye to Juliana, Gina got in the car and left. She had thought about Michael, and she asked herself how he would have felt knowing that she was going away for three days with Paul. She remembered that Michael used to complain about Paul and how competitive they used to get against each other on every work project they did together. She had decided to accept the invite for the chance of leaving the house for a while and having a break. Everything was getting too complicated at that point, and she hadn't had any time to herself since Michael passed away.

Also, Harry's visions were getting even more frequent.

Sometimes he would say that he had seen an angel in the room and sometimes he would start to scream, saying that he had seen a man in black surrounding the house. Gina took Harry to the doctors, but after doing several exams the results didn't point to anything being wrong with the boy. The trip with Paul had come at the right time, as Gina was becoming more and more stressed.

Half an hour later she arrived at Heathrow Airport. To her surprise, Paul was there waiting in the car park. He had an envelope as a gift in one hand and his luggage in the other.

—Hi Gina, you look very pretty – even more than usual.

Gina blushed and thanked him for the compliment. Paul then gave her the gift and asked her to open it.

Gina opened the gift and found tickets to a five-star hotel spa in Austria. They would be flying in less than two hours. Flattered by the surprise, Gina smiled and hugged Paul.

—What a nice surprise, Paul. I am speechless. I am so happy!

—You don't need to say anything. Let's hurry. We don't want to miss our flight. Let me carry your luggage.

Paul got hold of a trolley and placed their luggage on it. They walked inside the airport and, after the usual checks, eventually got on the plane.

Hours later they arrived in Austria and a chauffeur drove them to the lovely centre of Pörtschach where the hotel was located by the shore of Wörthersee. From the hotel they had a stunning view of Austria and the Southern Alps. At the front of the hotel by the lake, swans were swimming. The view was breathtaking.

—I've booked two separate rooms, Gina, so you don't have to worry about anything. My intention was to bring you here to relax and enjoy some quiet time. We are having three days in the peaceful surroundings of the Alps.

Paul dropped her at her room so she could get herself settled in and then went to his.

They met one hour later in the hotel lobby and went for a walk to explore the hotel and the surroundings. They strolled through the hotel's gardens

—OK, said Paul. Now is the time to forget about London, home, kids, the problems and everything. Let's relax. I have a few surprises planned for this weekend and I hope you will enjoy them. I think we had better start with an early lunch.

—I agree, said Gina smiling. I am actually feeling quite hungry.

Gina could see, not far from where they were standing in the garden, a beautifully decorated table with two chairs, and a waiter standing nearby.

—You had this planned, too? asked Gina.

—Yes, I thought we would be hungry after the early start, so I booked a special table in the garden for us.

The waiter greeted them and presented them with the menu. Everything was very romantic; the table had flowers, porcelain dishes and silver cutlery. The day was also helping to make the scene even more romantic. The temperature was mild, typical of May, and the sky was blue with only a few clouds. They had their lunch, and, as Paul had suggested, they didn't talk about anything to do with back home. His eyes were fixed on hers at all times. Even though it felt wrong, Gina had feelings for Paul that she had never felt before – it was as if they had a very similar energy. Since Michael had passed away Paul had been very present, making her feel totally secure.

Back at home after the school visit, Michael was walking in circles, looking very worried and perturbed. He was neurotically talking to himself and feeling angrier and angrier.

—How could God allow that to happen to me? How could God allow that man to do what he did?

Michael was getting more and more upset. He went outside to the back garden and, screaming insults at God, he kneeled down on the grass and cried with anger.

Harriet appeared next to him.

—What has happened, Michael? You seemed so fine this afternoon when I left you. You have been recovering your astral memory and remembering so many important things about yourself. How can you be so full of bad energy and anger?

—I remember, now, mother. I remember what he did to me, that man, that horrible man. On that morning at the TV station I was tired after doing the live coverage of the election vote-counting throughout the night. I went to the canteen on the sixth floor to make myself a cup of coffee and he came after me. Paul started to provoke me by saying that that had been the worst live journalistic coverage we had ever done. He was the chief editor and my boss, and I was so tired of his insults and his bossy way that I told him that I had had enough. I had received an offer to present the news in the US, and although I wasn't very keen to move, I decided then to accept. I told him about the job proposition and that I hadn't told Gina, though I was sure she would understand and agree that it would be a good move for our family. I quit the job right there in the staff canteen.

Michael started to cry and became very agitated.

Harriet tried to calm him.

—Don't get yourself so agitated. Your negative thoughts are making you confused and you're not seeing the reality.

58

Not changing his tone of voice, Michael continued.

—When I turned my back and went to the stairs he called me, and when I looked at him he pushed me down the stairs ...

Michael got so emotional that he couldn't speak anymore.

—It wasn't like that, son. I was there with you all the time. Stop the dark thoughts or they will only delay your progress.

Michael was crying and feeling angrier.

—Why didn't you protect me? Why did you let me die?

Feeling sorry for him, Harriet didn't say anything. Michael pushed her arms away when she tried to embrace him. Mateo appeared in the garden.

—We could not intervene in God's will, he told Michael firmly. We could not stop your passage. We could send positive vibes; we could protect you from feeling the pain that that violent fall caused you. Harriet could be there when you did the passage from the material world to our spiritual world, but in order to do anything we need authorisation from our superiors. And the truth is that was the time of your return home.

Michael was about to shout out loud once again, but he was stopped by Mateo, who carried on talking.

—Your energy right now doesn't belong to this place. Here there are only spirits who are searching for their soul's evolution. Your energy vibration is too bad right now, Michael. You will have to be sent to a different colony where you can get some comfort and get some special care. Your soul is still too hurt.

While Mateo was talking, Michael started to feel a calm and light feeling, and he had no power to speak.

—There you won't be able to see me or Harriet, Mateo continued, as it is a recovery clinic and our presence there won't be of any benefit to you, though we will always be looking after you ...

Mateo's voice had faded away completely in the air and Michael's vision turned fuzzy.

When Michael woke up he was in a different place. He was in a garden and at the end of the garden he could see a big and tall manor house. There was a water fountain in the middle of the garden. The fresh air was the same, though he could feel a difference in the energy of the place, as if it felt denser than at the Towers.

—Hello Michael.

Michael turned around and he could see a man looking at him.

—My name is Nathaniel and I will be your guardian angel while you are here at the recovery clinic. Here you will have classes on spirituality and learn more about who you are. You will learn more about the universe and its laws. Here we work too and we have a more regimented routine. You will find this place very different from the colony where you were before. Everybody who is here is going through some kind of problem, so the energy here is lower, which makes it very similar to the energy on planets like the earth. All the feelings and thoughts of the souls here are similar to earth because of the level of the spirits' evolution. The only difference is that everyone here is after spiritual evolution.

—Do you mean that I have stepped down?

—Not necessarily. Yes, this is an inferior colony as it reflects the energy of those inhabiting it. This place reflects exactly the same energy you are bringing with you. We attract to ourselves spirits and places with similar energy to ours; therefore you could not be at such a high-level spiritual colony any longer, as your energy right now is attracting bad vibrations.

—I need to go back to earth; I need to see my family. I know that

60

Paul is around my family and I need to stop him.

—Calm down, Michael. You can't intervene in their lives. It's Gina's decision to be around him and not yours. Your obsessive behaviour will only bring pain and confusion to you and to those around you. Try to think about good memories. Try to relax and remember to trust God's plan.

Michael thought, *It's better not to argue or say anything else. It doesn't matter what I say; they will keep on telling me to keep quiet. I need to find a way to go back to earth ...*

Nathaniel interrupted his thoughts.

—We can all read each other's thoughts. We no longer need to communicate using our vocal cords; they are instruments used only when you have a human body. Here we can all just communicate through thoughts. You are free to stay and you are also free to go. I can't keep you here as a prisoner. We can all show you the way, but only you can decide to walk towards it. If you wish to go back to earth you can, and so you are free to do so. I need to alert you to the fact that there are a lot of dark forces there. There are a lot of primitive spirits who decided to go against God's laws and to live there among those incarnated trying to create pain and suffering. Once you are there you will be among those various forces and energies.

—I am thankful for all your help, but I want to go back there. I want to be with my family and watch out for them. I can't stay here any longer.

Nathaniel looked at him, feeling very sorry for his decision.

—I must warn you about one last thing, he said. The lower the energy you get yourself involved with, the more difficult your way back here will be. Just as God gives us the free will to choose our paths, we are at the same time responsible for the consequences of our actions.

Goodbye now, Michael.

Chapter VIII
Two Enemies Reunited

Michael felt a hard, bad pain in his chest, and he closed his eyes as a reflection of the pain. The pain got worse and worse, and suddenly he could hear an enormous burst of sound. He had been so used to the peace and harmony of having no sound pollution that now even the sound of children in the playground was very disturbing. He looked around and found himself in a village that seemed to be somewhere in Europe. There were children playing at a playground near him and he was finding it difficult to stand the noise coming from everywhere. He looked around and he didn't recognise the place. *Is this another sort of spiritual clinic or spiritual colony?* he wondered.

He decided to walk and explore the place, and he saw that there was a lake not far from where he was. He walked in the direction of the lake, feeling something strange. He didn't know it, but he was being guided by his intuition. When he reached the lake he could visualise Gina sitting down on a bench admiring the view. He smiled and felt happiness again; there she was looking as good as always.

Michael ran over to her and started to shout her name. She didn't hear him. He shouted even louder, but there was no sign of Gina reacting to it. She carried on looking at the lake, not noticing that Michael was at that point hugging her.

—Gina, I am here, I am back! Look at me, I am back!

Michael shed tears of sadness when he realised that Gina could not hear or see him.

—I have missed you so much. I can't stop thinking about being with you again. I miss your smell; I miss your feel, your touch. I think about the way you used to look at me and how good you used to make me feel even after the longest and most stressful days at work. I miss you, dear.

Gina didn't reply, she couldn't reply. She suddenly started to change her thoughts and she then started to remember Michael. Within minutes she was filled with sorrow and sadness.

When Michael realised that Gina had changed her thoughts and had started to remember him, he realised that his presence had had an impact on her. Michael then embraced Gina even tighter.

—I'll never leave you again, he said crying. I am here and I will stay with you and the kids.

That sad feeling that had taken over Gina had become stronger and suddenly she too was crying.

Michael was taken by surprise when he heard Paul's voice.

—Why are you crying? said Paul, arriving with two ice creams.

Paul held her close and gave her a hug, which made Michael fall on the floor.

—Don't cry, baby. You are too pretty to be crying. Forget it right now, any kind of bad thoughts. Let's focus on our wonderful time together.

Michael was watching the scene from the floor, speechless and feeling a mixture of different feelings.

Paul saw an opportunity now that Gina was feeling vulnerable.

—Gina, I need to confess something to you; I haven't been honest with you. I never told you, but the day that I was with Michael in the ambulance, on the way to the hospital, he said something to me. He told me that he considered me as if I was the brother he never had and he asked me to look after you and the kids. I couldn't even think about replying to such a stupid question, but I guess he knew at that time that

64

he was dying. That's why I have been so close to you and the kids all this time, because of Michael's wish. But also because I am in love with you, Gina.

Gina felt confused at such a revelation and didn't know what to say.

—I know Michael and I had our arguments, but, Gina, they were all professional arguments. Arguments that we all have with our work colleagues. Michael knew that, and every time he had something bothering him he would ask me to go for a drink, and then he used to tell me his problems and ask for advice. He told me before he died that he had received a job offer from a TV channel in the US and he didn't know how to broach the subject with you. I felt so happy for him and we even did a toast to celebrate. I loved Michael as my best mate, and I know Michael would be happy for me to be with you and help you to look after the kids.

Michael stood up and very angrily started to shout.

—Liar! You liar! You were never my friend. You have killed me, you monster! Stay away from her.

Michael jumped on top of him and started to punch him. Suddenly Paul started to feel a pain on his chest, and he stopped breathing. He fell backwards on the floor and Gina, not knowing what to do, started to shout for help. Soon a couple that was walking nearby came to find out what had happened. The man started to massage Paul's chest and his girlfriend called the emergency services.

The ambulance came minutes later and the paramedics started to treat him. The ambulance took him to the nearest hospital and Gina went with him. Sitting inside the ambulance also was Michael.

Five days later, Paul was lying in a hospital bed and Gina was sitting in the chair next to him. Michael was also there watching over him. The place was quiet. It was the middle of the night and most of the patients were asleep. Gina and Paul were still sleeping when Michael heard a voice.

—Hey you, what are doing here?

It was a man with a long beard, dressed in an old dark suit, who had just come in.

—Are you talking to me? Michael replied, feeling surprised that he could be seen by someone else.

—Yes, I am talking to you. What are you doing here?

—I am watching over this man. He is trying to get involved with my wife and I can't allow this to happen.

The man took a look at Paul.

—Yeah, he looks like a horrible man. My name is Tomas – nice to meet you. By the way, I am dead too.

Michael thought that comment was funny. He smiled back at him.

—And my name is Michael and I am dead too.

The old man laughed.

—So, dead Michael, would you like to go for a walk? Don't worry about leaving him. It seems like he won't be going anywhere for now.

Michael accepted the invitation and they walked along the corridor of the small and quiet hospital.

—So, Tomas, I told you what I am doing here at the hospital. Now tell me, what brings you here?

—I am waiting for revenge. I am also waiting for a man. He is in his final days; I can see it coming. I'll get him back for all he has done to me.

At that moment Michael could see the man was surrounded by a dark shadow. The vibration coming from the man was becoming more and more negative.

—What did he do to you? asked Michael. What did he do in order to make you wait for him to die?

—He took away what I loved most in life; he took away my beloved wife, Liana. His name was Kurt Dollfuss, and he was a Nazi. I had just got married to the love of my life when they invaded our house, many of them. We were caught by them and sent to concentration camps. I have never seen her since. He was the leader of that group. He was the one who tortured me, and I could never forget what I have seen. Unlike many people I managed to escape the camps. I lived in hiding for the rest of the war, and when the Nazi regime came to an end I spent all my life looking for Liana, and for him. I found out after many years and many searches that Liana died in the concentration camp. And this man was the man who coordinated the concentration camp she was tortured in. I then spent my entire life searching for him. I died around ten years ago and only then did I find out that he was here in Austria, living under a different identity. I have been tormenting him and making his life a hell until now.

—What about your wife? Why didn't you reunite after you died?

—I met her briefly. Liana was there waiting for me when I died. She looked different and she spoke differently too. She was talking about forgiveness and saying that she had forgiven all of those who did this to us and our people. I tried hard to convince her that the best thing would be revenge, to torture him as he had tortured all of us, but she said she had found the light and was looking for her soul's elevation. She took me to a recovery colony, or something like that, and told me that we could not be together if I was still holding anger inside me.

—I guess if you loved her you would forgive this man and forget

67

about the past in order to spend eternity with her, wouldn't you?

Tomas's voice changed to a more aggressive tone.

—It has nothing to do with loving Liana, he replied. I cannot forgive this monster! I refused to stay in the spiritual colony and came back to earth for revenge. I found him and since then I have been surrounding him and everyone around him, sending as many dark thoughts and as much dark energy as I can. He says he regrets his past and has turned to Jesus and all of that, but I can never forgive him for what he did. I became his worst nightmare. I've learnt how to connect with him whilst he is asleep, and since then I started to appear in his dreams at night. So far I haven't managed to provoke much damage apart from some headaches and stomach pains now and then. My plan is to catch him when he dies.

—Have you heard from Liana again?

—I never heard from her again. They won't allow me where she is and I guess she now avoids me.

—So what's the point of all of this if you are still away from the one you love the most?

—I guess I am here for the same reason as you. Revenge, my friend, revenge!

Tomas stopped for a while and it seemed as if he was feeling something different. He apologised and said that he had to go back to the room where Kurt Dollfuss was.

—Excuse me, Michael. The moment I have been waiting for has finally arrived; he is about to die. I can feel it!

Tomas disappeared in the air.

While walking back to the room where Gina and Paul were, Michael heard a big noise and a scream. He followed the noise and suddenly he saw a very bright light coming out of a room. He got closer and when he walked through the door he saw Tomas on his knees, crying desperately. A woman with curly ginger hair and pale skin was there next to him. The woman had a very bright energy surrounding her spirit, similar to the light Harriet and Mateo had. Her light was brightening the entire room. There also in the room was the spirit of Kurt Dollfuss holding hands with two other spirits.

—Don't do this, Liana, cried out Tomas. I need to get my revenge!

—Enough of this rage, Tomas. You need to forget the past and forgive. You need to move on. This poor soul asked for forgiveness years ago. God has given him another chance and now he is going with us to a place where he is going to learn about his mistakes. You're not entitled to judge anyone!

Tomas screamed angrily at Kurt's spirit. Liana spoke to Tomas for the last time.

—If one day you clean yourself from this darkness that you have chosen to surround yourself with, you know what to do. Pray, and help will come to take you back home.

Liana disappeared together with the other two spirits who were holding Kurt's hands. When they left, the room went dark again. Doctors and nurses rushed to the room to help the man without knowing that he had already returned home.

Tomas remained on the floor looking lost and speechless.

—Are you okay? asked Michael.

—I can't believe that this is it. They took him and I couldn't even get close to him. I could not even stop them. So many years following that damn man, so much time and energy I put into waiting for this day, and now he is gone ...

Tomas looked devastated. Michael left the room and went back to check on Paul. While on his way to Paul's room he could still hear Tomas crying.

When he got back to the room he found Gina lying across Paul's bed, embracing him.

—I'll take you home soon, Paul, she said.

—I am so glad that you're here with me, said Paul, stroking her hand. It's so good to have you here. You've been an angel to me. Now tell me, how are the kids doing?

—Don't worry about the kids. They are fine. Isabel and Juliana are looking after them. They have both been my angels. I have been talking to them every day on the phone, so don't worry. It's all fine. Just, please, get yourself better soon so we can go back home.

—You haven't said anything about what I said to you that day by the lake. I don't want to force anything, but I am sure about my love for you, Gina.

Gina blushed and didn't say anything for a while.

—It's all very new for me, Paul. Don't get me wrong, please. I appreciate your company and I really enjoy spending time with you. Sometimes I wonder how I would have gone through all of this without Isabel, Juliana and you in my life. Let's take it easy for now. Let's get you better soon and go back to London before we start to think about anything else.

—Sorry, but you've lost me now. Does that mean that I have a chance or not?

She smiled.

—Yes, you do, she said softly.

Michael was in panic watching everything. His wife was there in front of his eyes exchanging kind words with a man he hated. He felt angry and betrayed. Negative thoughts were going through his mind.

How could she forget me so quickly? Full of anger he started to punch Paul on his chest. He thought that as it had worked before at the lake, perhaps it could work again. He knew that somehow he could inflict pain on Paul. Michael punched him even harder, but when he was just about to get hold of his neck to strangle him, Michael was dragged backwards with such strength that he flew across the room, falling flat on the floor. Before he could recover from the fall, he was forcibly kicked. Suffering from an intense pain his vision went fuzzy and all he could see were dark shadows surrounding him. He tried to get up off the floor, but as he did one of the dark shadows punched him in the face. His vision went fuzzy again, and not being able to stand the pain any longer he fell unconscious. The dark shadows laughed out loud, and when they realised he was unconscious they left the room.

Chapter IX
Back in London

When Michael woke up he did not know what had happened to him. He took a look around and to his surprise Gina and Paul were no longer there. There was an old lady on the bed where Paul had been and people whom he assumed to be her family and relatives around her. He was feeling confused and his head felt heavy. He could hear somebody calling his name.

—Michael, are you OK?

It was Tomas.

—I don't know what happened, replied Michael. Where did they go, Gina and that monster?

I saw them leaving the hotel about two days ago. You have been there all this time. I tried to wake you up, but they were very strong and they threatened me.

—Who? Who did this to me?

—They were three black men. I saw them watching the room from outside. They followed your wife and that man when they left. They were not good. They have very dark energies.

—Why didn't I see them before?

—I don't know why, but I know that they have very angry faces. I got the feeling that they were with him. I tried to read their minds but for some reason I couldn't.

—I need to find Gina, Tomas. She is in danger. I need to go to London now.

—I can take you there and show you how to go anywhere you want. Empty your mind and all you have to think of now is where you would like to go. Now hold my hands and I'll take you there.

Michael held Tomas's hands and they disappeared in the air.

They reappeared in Richmond, right inside Michael's old living room. Juliana the babysitter was reading a book to Kit and Grace while Harry was playing on the computer. Michael was amazed at how they could have travelled in a matter of less than a second all the way from Austria to his living room. He stared at his kids, who were nearly falling asleep listening to Juliana's story. He stood speechless for a while, watching the three of them. Michael moved closer to his kids and observed every detail in their expressions; he tried to smell them and even tried to touch them. He smiled while watching the kids. Kit the youngster had his hair longer now and with his blonde hair and dark blue eyes was a mixture of Michael and Gina. Grace had curly, dark blonde hair and green eyes, very similar to Gina. Harry was the one who impressed Michael the most. Harry was becoming more and more similar to him when he was a kid, with light ginger hair and blue eyes. While he was watching Harry playing his game on the computer, he noticed that Harry stopped playing the game to open a folder on the computer where all the family photos were. Harry went through the pictures without noticing that his father was there right beside him, looking at each picture with him. Harry then found a picture that showed his father hugging him. Michael noticed that at that point, while staring at the picture, Harry's eyes filled up with tears. The boy put his hand on the computer screen as if trying to touch his father. Michael couldn't hold back his tears.

When Juliana realised that Harry had started to cry, she left the other two children, who had fallen asleep on the sofa, and went over to Harry, hugged him, and sang a song to him in Portuguese.

Harry fell asleep in her arms while she sang to him. Feeling sad,

Michael embraced his son and continued to cry.

Sensing Michael's presence, Juliana spoke to the boy while he was asleep.

—Dad has to know that he needs to go back with the angels, because this is not his place anymore. We are all fine ...

Michael was scared by what Juliana had just said.

—Can you see me, Juliana? Talk to me? I know you can, so talk to me!

Juliana, who was still holding Harry in her arms, started to pray in silence.

Michael carried on talking to her.

—I need you to say something to Gina. I need you to give her a message.

Juliana carried on praying, and before Michael could continue the entire living room was filled by a very bright light. An old black lady appeared from behind Juliana, brightening the entire room.

—She is a medium, the lady said to Michael. So she could sense your presence here and she could also hear you, because that's her gift in this life. But she can only hear what God allows her to hear, and I am afraid that she couldn't hear the message you just tried to deliver to Gina.

—Who are you? asked Michael.

—I am her mentor. I watch over her and visit her when she calls my name. Juliana and I do spiritual work together. Once a week we meet at the same spiritual home to help spirits in need, just like you.

—I am not in need. I am only caring for my family. They are in danger and I am here to protect them.

—You don't protect anyone – only God can. I am afraid that the more and more you distance yourself from God, the more difficult things will get for you.

—If you are here to preach, I am afraid you have wasted your time. I have made my decision and I am staying with my family.

—We know this, Michael. I am not here to interfere with your decision. I am here for your friend.

—What friend?

—Tomas. Come here, son.

Tomas moved closer to the lady and went down on his knees.

The lady put her hands over Tomas's head.

—You called for God and your prayer has been answered, Tomas, she said. I am here in the name of our Lord for you. It's time to return home.

Michael looked admiringly at Tomas.

—Why have you cried for help? Michael asked him.

—When I saw your kids playing and how happy you were when you saw them again, I began to pray. I asked for forgiveness.

Tomas looked at the old woman before continuing.

—I want to return home. I want to go back to the colony.

The lady closed her eyes and two tall angels with long wings appeared in the room. At that point Tomas was shedding tears and he was visibly tired. One of the angels picked him up. Its wings embraced Tomas and the angel carried him with the softness of a parent carrying a newborn baby. Both angels walked away and disappeared in the air.

The old woman put her hands around Juliana's head and prayed for her. Once she finished praying, she turned to Michael.

—You can always return, Michael. This isn't your place anymore. Don't think that you are protecting someone here, because you're not. Life goes according to our Lord's will and no one can change. Being here will only bring you pain and confusion. I can take you back with me if you want?

Michael looked at his kids, who were asleep on the couch, and then at Harry, who was still sleeping in Juliana's arms.

—No, he replied. I will stay and watch over my family. Gina is in danger and I need to protect her even though you're trying to convince me otherwise.

—This is your choice. As you learnt, we have our free will and no one can go against that. Gina is only having the consequences of her own choices, and no one can intervene – not even you, Michael. We have consequences for every decision we make in life. Juliana won't be able to hear you as I am going to be protecting her. One day, when the time is right, Gina will know the truth and you will understand why things are now the way they are. I am going now, son. I hope you come back home soon.

The old woman left the room. The kids were still asleep and Juliana was feeling calmer. Michael was immobile, staring into empty space, thinking about what he had just heard. He liked the things he had learnt while in the colony in the company of Harriet and Mateo. He also missed the peaceful feeling he felt when he was there. He started to contemplate the thought of returning there with Gina and his kids. His thoughts were interrupted by a familiar voice coming through the room; it was Gina, who had got home with Isabel.

—Oh Isabel, said Gina. Come and take a look at these little angels sleeping.

Gina dropped her bag on the floor and bent towards the sofa where Kit and Grace were sleeping. She stroked their heads.

—I could never live without these little babies, she said. Look how cute they are. Harry is growing so fast. He looks more and more like Michael every day.

Michael smiled at this.

—Talking about Michael, said Isabel, may I ask you about Paul? How are you feeling now? And what are you going to say next time you see him?

—I don't know. We're supposed to meet up tonight. He is coming here and we are going to watch a movie. I don't know how to feel about it. I love Michael and I think of him every day. I look at Harry and he reminds me of his smile, his smart eyes ... Michael was my first love, but ...

—But?

—But he is dead, now, and I need to carry on with my life, don't I?

She seemed very confused.

A sad feeling took over Michael. Although he knew that Gina would have to move on with her life eventually, Paul was the last person he wanted to see Gina getting herself involved with.

Before Isabel could say any more, the kids woke up and Juliana came into the room. Kit and Grace started to scream with delight when they saw their mum and Isabel, and gave them big hugs, although Harry seemed tired and upset. Juliana explained to Gina that the kids had fallen asleep and that she had taken the opportunity to do some ironing in the bedroom.

While Gina was talking to the kids and playing with them, Juliana called Isabel aside and asked her to go to the kitchen.

—I am a little bit worried, Isabel.

—What happened? I can see that you look a little bit pale. Are you OK?

—About an hour ago I was playing with the kids. I saw Harry looking at some pictures on the computer. Suddenly he began to cry while staring at a picture of his father. I went over to give him a hug and talk to him and suddenly I could see Mr Michael by his side. He looked sad and he didn't seem to be OK. Harry was completely sad and I guess it was due to his father's presence near him. Harry could sense the negative energy that Mr Michael was carrying with him. I could feel it and I tell you now that Mr Michael's energy wasn't good. I know he is suffering.

Isabel had started to learn about spiritism after being invited by her French boyfriend, who was a student at the same spiritual home as Juliana. It had been Isabel who had recommended Juliana to Gina after meeting her at the spiritual centre.

—And what did you do when you saw him? asked Isabel.

—I told him that he should leave because this isn't his place anymore. I started to pray to my spiritual guide and angels for protection. After I prayed I could feel my spiritual guide around me and then I could not see Michael anymore. I can feel he is still here, but I cannot see him.

—You need to tell Gina; she needs to know. If you tell her, she might finally lose the fear and go with us to the spiritual centre.

—She won't believe me. You know how she feels about these things. She makes jokes out of it and deep down she feels scared. I know she won't do it. I also feel scared that such a subject could make her upset, and then she could end up firing me.

—Don't be silly, Juliana. She wouldn't fire you just for that reason, though I know what you mean. Let's figure out a way to talk to her. Whatever happens I can guarantee she won't sack you. Don't worry about that.

Isabel lowered her voice before carrying on.

—For now I am worried about something else, someone who's

alive.

—Why? What is happening?

—I think Gina is falling in love with Paul.

—This is really good for her, said Juliana giggling. She needs to move on ...

Before she could continue, Gina came into the room holding Kit in her arms, followed by Grace and Harry.

—What are you two up to? she said smiling.

—We are planning a day to meet at the spiritual centre. I haven't been for a meeting in ages, so I was asking Juliana to let me know the next time she goes so we can go together.

—I have told you two so many times, said Gina. Leave the dead where they are. Anyway, I am going to check Harry's homework. Juliana, could you stay with Kit and Grace for a while please?

Juliana smiled and nodded.

Michael had been watching over Gina and the kids, and so he had missed the conversation between Juliana and Isabel in the kitchen. He was still feeling sad after all he had heard. How could Gina believe in such lies? He felt betrayed by her for not trusting his love for her.

Isabel kissed all the kids goodbye, said goodbye to Juliana, wished Gina good luck with the date later on and left.

Later on that evening, when the kids were getting ready to go to bed and Gina was finishing getting ready to go out to the cinema, Juliana plucked up the courage to speak to Gina about what had happened earlier on in the day.

—I know you have told me lots of times that you don't believe in life after death, but I swear to you that I saw Mr Michael in the living room this afternoon. He looked very angry and upset, but I couldn't understand what he was trying to say.

When she heard Michael's name Gina felt goosebumps and her heart started to beat faster. Michael was by her side at that moment and he started to stroke her hair. He cried, feeling a mixture of feelings; he was feeling sad as he was missing her but feeling at the same time betrayed because of her involvement with Paul.

—I would like you to come with me to a meeting at the spiritual centre, Juliana went on. Even though you don't believe, please, do it for me.

Gina, who had been crying, dried her tears.

—You have probably been talking to Isabel too much. The dead are dead and they won't come back. Let's leave them alone! Although I do respect your beliefs, please don't mention this again to me. I am sorry for being rude; I am just trying to be happy again. Please forgive me.

She gave Juliana a hug.

—Please put the kids to sleep for me. I'll see you tomorrow for breakfast.

Still feeling upset and confused, Michael didn't think twice and followed Gina. Deep down a fear of facing Paul again was taking over him, this time deeper than ever. Michael followed Gina outside and with a lot of pain he witnessed their very brief kiss followed by a hug. He had not noticed at that stage the dark spirits sitting in the back of the car. Gina sat in the front seat of the car and Michael got into the back. He was taken by surprise when he noticed that two black men were sitting next to him.

—Hello, hello! said the two men at the same time, both being very sarcastic.

—Who are you? asked Michael with fear in his voice. And what are you doing here?

—Don't you remember us?

The man grabbed Michael by his arm.

—He hasn't recovered his astral memory yet, said the other man. How come?

Gina and Paul were talking and laughing, unaware that the two spirits were being aggressive to Michael in the back seat.

—Now I remember, said Michael. You were there in that private hospital in Austria, weren't you? It was you who attacked me on that day at the hospital. What do you want from me?

The two men grabbed Michael's arms and closed their eyes. The three of them disappeared in the air.

Chapter X
The Slave's Plan

—Where are we now? Where did you bring me to? asked Michael, trying to get away from the two guys.

—Look around; you should be able to recognise this place. We brought you to Liverpool. We are now going to finally be able to teach you a lesson!

The other man continued.

—We want revenge. You're going to pay back every drop of blood that your family took from our people.

Michael didn't understand anything they were saying. He thought it would be better not to say anything.

—You should remember how much pain you and your father caused all of us. You and your father have our blood on your hands. You were slave traders and built a massive fortune capturing Africans like us and selling us all over the world. You separated so many families by sending members of the same family to different countries. Older people used to be killed as a way to show the youngest how they could be punished if they didn't obey; children were tortured and used as slaves and servants in the houses of rich people. Others were sent to farms around the Americas, working long hours under the hot sun and hardly being able to raise a family. The Worley family used to send their staff to hunt my people and torture those who were brave enough to fight against them. All the money you earned was dirty with our people's blood. Even now, so many years after the slave trade came to an end, my people still carry in their souls the brutal marks of those times. The Worley family caused us too much pain through the years and now we want revenge.

—You are wrong … You've got the wrong guy. I am Michael, I never hurt anyone … If you are talking about that experience in Liverpool, it wasn't me! I was Jonathan … I was against all of that …

—Shut up! shouted one of the men.

They dragged Michael inside a derelict house and once they got inside the house they threw him into a corner. They tied his legs with a long chain linked to a heavy metal ball.

—You are making a mistake, you've got the wrong man! Paul … My cousin Paul is the man you are after. He was Peter Wor–

Michael was interrupted again.

—Listen. We have been after you and your family for many years. You escaped twice but won't escape again. Your father is the next on our list. If those damn people hadn't taken him away, we would have been able to make him pay. But now that he is reincarnated again they won't be able to help him.

—Why are you around my family? What do you want with my family?

Both men laughed out loud.

—You haven't got a clue what's going on, have you? We want your father, and it's just a matter of time until we get our hands on him. There are many of us on this case and we are following orders from our leader. We will keep you as our prisoner here until we manage to get your father.

—And by the way, the other man added. You'd better not try to escape. There's nothing you can do to go and see your family. We are stalking them until we get the boy.

84

—Boy? What are you talking about? Leave my wife and my kids alone. My kids have nothing to do with your business.

Michael stood up and went for the throat of one of the men.

—Leave my family alone! he shouted.

The taller of the two guys pulled him off and threw him back on the floor. They were very strong and Michael realised he couldn't fight them. He felt his energy drain away, and he had no power to stand up or even move.

—Are you stupid? Have you forgotten our strength? We are much stronger than you ...

The taller guy punched Michael and leaned in close to his face.

—You'd better listen very carefully and follow our orders; otherwise, your wife and kids will pay. We are constantly around them, and trust me we can cause them a lot of damage.

—We will get revenge on you once we have got hold of your father. For now we will give you a task. Look around – see that girl?

The house was covered with rubbish. There were old papers everywhere and empty cans of lager all over the place. There was a little black girl of about seven years old. She was sitting on the floor surrounded by all that mess; she was holding a dirty doll. The doll she was holding looked more like an old piece of rubbish than a child's toy. The girl was playing with the doll and tidying her hair. Next to the girl was her mother, who was sleeping on the sofa.

Michael was watching the little girl and at the same time he was feeling sorry for her.

—Her name is Gabrielle, explained one of the men. She is only seven. Her father is an alcoholic and her mother is abused by him on a daily basis. Gabrielle spends the whole day watching TV, playing with her only doll and hoping her father doesn't come back home drunk.

—I feel sorry for her just by looking at her, said Michael. But what do you want me to do? My life is a mess. I can only think of my family, and I cannot see how I can help this little creature.

—You're forbidden to get closer to your family. If you do so your children will pay the price. We will send so much dark energy to them that they will fall very ill and they won't survive. Obey us and your family will be fine ... Well, at least two of the children. There's no salvation for the boy. If you don't follow the rules, we will get them too. Follow our orders and everything will be fine.

—Yes, I'll obey, Michael replied.

—Good. You're not as stupid as we thought. We will leave you here for now and will return to let you know what we expect from you. For now just observe the family and don't even think of trying to escape. We will be able to track you down wherever you go. Your chain is monitored by us. It's long enough for you to go anywhere in the house, but it won't allow you to leave the house.

—I am afraid I am not the best one to do this job; my mind is a mess right now. I insist you have got the wrong man ... Paul is there, free, you should go after him! I will help you to get revenge on him if you wish, but please, let me go and be with my family ...

—Shut up! Be quiet here and just do as you have been told.

The two men started to get distant from him.

—Don't forget, Michael, that if you lose your control the consequences will be very complicated, not just for your family but also for Gabrielle. We are leaving now, but we will be back soon. If you need to call us, my name is Buziba, and my friend here is Enu.

The two men disappeared into the air.

Why do they think I am Peter? thought Michael. *I could never behave like that, would never have done such acts ... What do they want from me?* He watched Gabrielle playing with the doll.

His thoughts were interrupted by Oscar returning home. Oscar slammed the door, waking up the woman on the sofa.

—Did I wake you up? Go and make me dinner, because I am hungry! said Oscar.

Nina, his wife, seemed to be drunk, and tripped over the rubbish as she made her way to the kitchen.

Gabrielle stopped playing with the doll and looked at her father as if waiting for him to say something to her.

—Hey you, he said. Move your head away from the telly.

Michael was watching everything from the corner of the room, and more and more he started to feel sorry for Gabrielle. The energy around that house was very low and negative, and Michael was trying hard not to cry and get himself even more down. He knew that if he didn't follow the orders he had received, his family would be in trouble. Noticing that the little girl's face had changed to one of sadness, he walked towards her and sat down on the floor by her side. He put his hands close to her face and started to think about the spiritual colony he had once been in. He thought about the animals running wild around the field, the lakes and stunning views he had seen there, and the peaceful energy he had felt in that place. Suddenly Michael changed his own energy and he was able to inspire Gabrielle with his thoughts. She got hold of her doll and started to play again whilst Michael continued to heal his and her soul with positive thoughts.

After a while, and after Oscar had shouted at his wife many times to hurry up with the dinner, Nina entered the living room carrying two plates. She gave one to her husband and one to Gabrielle. The girl thanked her mother with a look of fear on her face and ate the food like someone who'd been starving for the whole day. Her father then looked at her and finally said his first nice words of the night to her.

—That was nice, ah? You are going to have to learn how to use the microwave soon so you don't need to rely on your lazy mother for food. You are too skinny. You will end up growing and becoming a stupid woman like your mother if you don't eat more.

He laughed as he said this.

Gabrielle didn't know what to say. She had learnt in her short life that her parents were very unstable and could change their mood very quickly, going from happy and playful to angry and aggressive in a matter of seconds.

Her mother swore at her father and lit a cigarette before leaving the room. Oscar fell asleep on the sofa straight after dinner. Gabrielle carried on playing with the doll for a while more, and then later in the evening she got herself a little blanket that had been left on the floor and went to her bedroom upstairs. She went to bed and covered herself up with the blanket, falling asleep. Michael, who had followed her every step, cried as he watched the girl going to sleep on her own, without anyone to look after her. Michael lay down by her side and, embracing her, sang the song he used to sing to his kids when tucking them in at night.

The following day, early in the morning, Michael woke up to the sound of Buziba and Enu shouting at Oscar.

—You need a drink ... You feel like you need a drink!

—Actually you need a stone. You desperately need a stone!

Even though Oscar couldn't see or hear the two spirits, influenced by their negative energy, he jumped out of bed and picked up a pipe that was on the bedside cabinet and lit up a stone of crack.

Buziba and Enu continued.

—Watch this lazy woman … She needs to get a job!

Oscar began to poke his sleeping wife, repeating the words of Buziba and Enu.

—Go and get a job, you bitch! Get up!

Oscar dragged her out of bed by her hair.

Buziba and Enu were laughing and seemed to be getting a lot of pleasure out of the situation. Oscar seemed to turn angrier the more he smoked. He slapped Nina, who was still half asleep, across the face. Nina gave him a slap back and they started to fight.

Michael had watched the whole scene, and by the time the two had reached the point of hurting each other, he realised that the noise had woken Gabrielle and that she too was watching. She stood between her parents and begged her father to stop.

—Stop, daddy; you are going to hurt mummy!

Oscar pushed his wife to the floor and left the room. Nina's body was aching and her lips were bleeding. Gabrielle ran to the bathroom and brought back a damp cloth to clean the blood from her mother's lips.

—Did you see, Michael, what we can do to your family? said Buziba still laughing.

—What do you want from this family? Why are you tormenting them?

—We want him, Enu replied. Oscar betrayed our leader and our mission is to make his life a misery. We have been tormenting him since he reincarnated. We are going to drive him to kill himself.

—What about Gabrielle and her mother? Why do you cause them suffering?

—We don't care about those two. We want him.

They were still laughing.

—It's funny to see the two ladies suffering, though, said Enu. Don't you think?

—Now listen to your job, slave, said Buziba. You've seen how our thoughts influenced his thoughts. We want you to send him bad vibrations, bad thoughts. We want to drive him to his limits until he cannot resist. We want his death to be slow and painful. He is already addicted to crack and it won't be long until he dies. Until then we want to cause him as much pain as we can. And as we have too many jobs to look after we will leave you here as our slave. You will torment him whenever we are not here.

—I cannot. This isn't right! I cannot cause this little child pain!

Buziba looked at him with a serious expression.

—If you don't want to see your family suffering, you have to.

—Before we leave, added Enu, don't forget that every time you fail to torment him, your family will pay!

They explained the plan to Michael, which consisted of focusing his thoughts on negative thoughts, the majority linked to the use of drugs and suicide. After explaining the plan they left. Michael for the first time regretted leaving the colony and leaving Mateo and Harriet. He leaned against the wall and cried, feeling sorry for himself.

Six months later

The situation in the house had got worse. Oscar had lost his job and was spending most of his time stoned on crack. He was spending most of the time high and behaving violently towards his wife. Michael looked very different. He had dark circles around his eyes; he seemed drained and had lost a lot of his energy due to the tormenting sessions he had engaged in with Oscar. Every time he sent negative thoughts towards Oscar to torment him it was as if somehow they acted on his spirit too. He could feel the bad energy he was sending to Oscar come back much stronger to him. Michael had to stop the sessions a few weeks after he started, as he had lost most of his energy. Buziba and Enu took over the job and tormented Oscar for nearly twenty-four hours. Michael could not move. He spent most of the time depressed, lying down on the floor. His spirit had turned black and dense. Gina and the kids were barely in his mind as he could not focus his mind anymore.

Oscar became heavily addicted to heroin and spent his last weeks begging in the streets, stealing or using drugs. He would rarely come back home. At that point he was completely surrounded by obscure and dark spirits.

One day when Gabrielle and Nina had both gone out, Oscar returned home and went straight to the bedroom. He could barely walk and his vision was completely fuzzy. Michael was lying on the floor, with no energy. That day Michael met the leader of the dark legion for the first time.

A very tall creature, different from anything Michael had ever seen, suddenly appeared in the bedroom. It had a very unpleasant smell and was wearing a cloak, making it difficult for Michael to distinguish its real shape and form. Dark shadows could be seen surrounding the very tall creature. The shadows were surrounding the tall being and going all around it in circles. Buziba and Enu were in the room along with many other inferior spirits. Some of them were addicted spirits who were attached to Oscar and benefited from his drug addictions, whilst other other inferior spirits belonged to the dark legion.

The creature didn't acknowledge Michael and went through him, going straight to the bed that Oscar was sitting on. The bad smell was so strong that Michael became paralysed. What Michael didn't know was that what he was feeling wasn't a smell but the negative and dark energy that the being carried with it. The leader of the dark legion got closer to Oscar and shouted at him.

—Die, you bastard! You are nothing! You have never been a real man. Life can be much better without scum like you. Society will be much better without you, die!

Immediately Oscar seemed to go into a trance. He became afflicted and his heart started beating faster. He was having a panic attack. Oscar went through his bedside cabinet and searched all the drawers. He took a syringe out and, with his hands shaking, he then prepared the heroin.

The leader of the dark legion continued.

—You have to die to come to me and pay your debts. Traitor. Come on, inject! Your life is miserable because you are nothing. Inject the heroin ...

He laughed out loud when Oscar injected the drug into his veins. At that point the dark shadows around the leader of the legion seemed to have got very excited and began to move, transferring towards Oscar's body. Oscar's eyes turned red, and his veins became visibly dark. After a few seconds his body started to shake. He fell flat on the bed. He had a convulsion.

His soul lifted up, still linked to his body by the bonds. Oscar's vision was fixed on his body, which was shaking on the bed. He was filled with panic. He was watching his own death. He looked around the room and saw Michael on the floor, scared, staring at him. On the other side he saw Buziba, Enu and all the other inferior and dark spirits. They were all looking at him as though he were their prey.

The leader of the dark legion looked down at him.

—It's only a matter of time before your bonds are completely broken. You will be dead soon.

Terrified, Oscar looked at him and at that point felt the bonds that linked his body and his soul break. His spirit was free from his human body. He was arrested by the spirits of the dark legion at the same instant as his corporeal body died.

—Bring the bastard! said the leader of the legion to all the other spirits who at that point were surrounding Oscar's soul.

He faced Michael.

—How do you feel being a prisoner now? I hope you enjoy your moments here as much as you can, because soon we will get hold of your father and then it will be time for the Worleys to pay back what they have done!

The leader of the legion and all the other spirits left. Michael was petrified on the floor. He had never seen such a scary scene before. Moments later the door slammed. Nina had returned home to find Oscar's dead body on the bed.

Michael closed his eyes. He could not face any more suffering. Whilst Nina screamed and tried to revive her husband, Michael covered his ears with his hands and called for God.

—Please Lord, help me!

Chapter XI
The Visions of Harry

Gina and Isabel met for lunch after Gina had called Isabel saying that she needed to talk to her. When Gina arrived at Isabel's house she looked terrified. Worried, Isabel asked her to go inside and offered her a cup of tea, which Gina promptly accepted.

—I needed so much to see you and talk to you, said Gina.

—What's going on? asked Isabel while boiling water for the tea.

—This is so embarrassing. I don't even know how to begin ...

—We are like sisters, Gina. Don't tell me that anything could be so horrible that you would be too embarrassed to talk to me about it. Now tell me, because you're making me worried. Spit it out!

—It's Harry ... I think he is losing it.

Gina looked so depressed when she said that that Isabel suggested they go to the living room to sit down on the sofa where they could talk more comfortably.

—I was called to the school yesterday again because of his behaviour. He is still talking about those dark men following him and surrounding our house. The situation has been getting worse since he began to say that those men have started to talk to him. Paul advised me to take him to see a friend of his who is a psychiatrist, and so Harry has been seeing him for over four weeks now.

—I thought he had stopped with all of that, because you never mentioned anything to me again.

—I just feel embarrassed about this whole thing. My little boy is losing his mind, acting like a madman. I was called yesterday to the school and the headmaster showed me drawings he has been doing in the class and I was shocked ...

She paused, taking a long breath before carrying on.

—He has been drawing pictures of a man pushing me down the stairs. There are several of them. In some pictures the man is killing me and Michael at the same time, in the other pictures Michael is already dead, covered in blood, with this man on top of him.

—Oh my God, Gina. How terrible!

—I know. He signed his name on all the pictures. The whole thing is so embarrassing. Of course they all said that they are very concerned about him and wanted to know what kind of precautions I am taking ...

She sighed and then carried on.

—Now I don't know what to do anymore. I feel scared of leaving him alone with Kit and Grace, because I don't know what's going on inside his head. I have to watch him twenty-four seven, and deep down I feel so lost. He has become aggressive towards everyone ...

—Calm down, Gina. First of all, you should not think about what the teachers or anyone else think about it. It's not time for any of them to judge you as a mother – they should be helping you get through this. Forget about other people's opinions and just think about him. Did you try and talk to him about the drawings?

—Yes. I did ask what he meant by them, and he said that those scary men who are now talking to him told him that he is going to die. They keep on telling him that he is a bad boy and many other things. I lost my temper with him after all this time and gave him a big shake. I shouted at him, telling him to stop creating stories. Then I felt bad for shouting at him and losing control, but I just don't know what to do ...

Gina started to cry.

—Michael left me here on my own, she went on. I now have to work and provide for the house on my own, look after the house on my own, look after three kids on my own, and plus I have to look after my son who seems to be going mental.

Gina cried for a while, with her hands covering her face, and Isabel, holding her, left her to cry as she knew that Gina needed to get all those bad feelings off her chest. After releasing all the stress, Gina felt a little bit calmer.

—Everything is going to be OK, Isabel assured her. You're very down, Gina, and I have never seen you like this before. You have beautiful kids and at least you have a very comfortable financial situation. You have Paul, who has been so supportive and caring ... I am sorry to say it, but you are being a bit overdramatic when you say that your whole life is collapsing. Now I agree with you that the situation with Harry is alarming, and he needs some extra care, and I promise to help you with this. But please focus on the positive things, and you will see that the more positive thinking you insert into your life, the better the problems will get.

Gina kept looking down while Isabel continued.

—You have always been so positive and full of energy! You have always been a strong woman. You lost a very important person in your life and Harry might be feeling lost too.

Still Gina did not say anything. Isabel continued.

—I know you have always refused my invites. This time I am not inviting but telling you to come with me to the spiritism meeting on Tuesday. I will pick you up at six o'clock – and no excuses.

—Tuesday is Juliana's night off, so I will have no one to look after the kids for me.

—I knew you would find an excuse. There is no problem, as they have a learning class for children there too, so you can take them with you. It will be good for Harry, as they do healing sessions for children. Invite Paul – I am sure he will appreciate the good energy from that place. You will find people there who are in search of peace.

—Well, I promise I will think about it. But please tell me more about this place.

—Amelia, the founder, hosts the meetings at a house she owns in North London. She converted the house specially to be able to run the meetings and do her charity work. We have the general meetings every Tuesday and Thursday evening for the general public. In the meetings we learn about *The Gospel According to Spiritism*, which is one of the five most important works by Allan Kardec. In this work he reviews some of the most fundamental teachings of Jesus and relates them to spiritism. Our doctrine follows his studies and his most fundamental works: *The Spirits Book*, *The Book of Mediums*, *The Genesis According to Spiritism*, *Heaven and Hell* and *The Gospel According to Spiritism*. At the spiritual home we also have weekly work classes for people with a better knowledge of spiritism and the works of Kardec.

—Wow. I guess I am overwhelmed with so much information.

—I understand you must be. Trust me – you will enjoy your visit.

The friends continued their conversation, and by the time Gina left she was feeling much more relieved and more able to face her challenges.

On the following day

Harry was in the classroom. The teacher was reading a short story and asked everyone to pay attention as they were going to discuss the story afterwards. Harry was holding his pencil tightly with both hands. His face was serious and he had an evil look in his eyes.

What no one in the classroom realised was the fact that two spirits with very dark shadows were surrounding Harry. They were feeding the boy thoughts of dark energy.

—We have finally found you. Did you think you were going to hide forever? said Buziba to Harry.

—You will suffer as you have never suffered before! Buziba continued tormenting him.

Enu grabbed the boy's ear and said "but before that we will have fun with you".

Harry began feeling agitated. His heart was beating fast, sweat started to drip down from his forehead and although he could not see his tormentors his spirit could sense their presence and their dark energy.

Suddenly the voices of Buziba and Enu became clear to Harry.

—We will make your mother and that 'softy' boyfriend of hers suffer. And do you know why? Because you don't deserve to have a nice family! You are a little bastard! Said Enu still grabbing his ear.

—No! Harry shouted.

His teacher and classmates were horrified.

–Leave me alone! Harry shouted.

At that instant all the children ran to the front of the classroom scared of his behaviour. In the meantime Harry continued to scream.

—Leave me alone!

The teacher dropped the book on the floor and went towards him.

—Harry! Who are you shouting at? The teacher asked.

Harry broke the pencil in half and shouted louder; they are after me Ms Johnson and they want to get my mother too!

Having fun with the situation; Buziba and Enu intensified the torment by screaming nonsense words in his ear creating more distress and confusion in his mind.

Harry stood up on his chair and continued to shout. With one of the hands he punched the teacher who tried to get hold of him. The kids remained in panic at the front of the classroom watching the scene in horror. Harry kicked the teacher whilst she tried to get hold of his arms. He kicked her and began to attack her with kicks and punches.

More Buziba and Enu screamed more distressed he turned into. He ran around the classroom screaming and grabbing the other children's belongings throwing everything in the air.

Suddenly the room brightened up and two other spirits arrived to calm down the situation. Laughing out loud Buziba and Enu left the room as soon as they realized the arrival of the two spirits. The teacher got hold of him once again and at the same time the two superior spirits that had arrived in the room started to pray with their hands over his head.

Feeling calmer but at the same time very vulnerable he shed tears whilst all the children began to call him bad names. The teacher took him outside the classroom asking the other children to return to their seats and wait for her.

—What has just happened Harry? Are you going insane? I am sorry but this was the last time... said the teacher taking him to the headmaster's office.

Gina arrived at the headmaster's within minutes after receiving the phone call from his secretary. She was feeling concerned about her son's mental health but also embarrassed as that was the fourth time she had been called because of Harry's misbehaviour.

—I am really sorry Ms Barker though I am afraid that since there's nothing wrong with your son's health I will have to classify this as a very severe incident. Being this the fourth time your son engage in violent and disorder behaviour I will have to expel him from school.

—Expel? What do you mean? Expel my son from the school...Is this how the school shows support and help?

99

—I am sorry Ms Barker, it's not a matter of supporting anymore. We are responsible for the other pupils too and I am afraid that your son's behaviour isn't...how I can say this in the nicest way...

—Oh I understand Mr Morrison. Please save me from your nice way of saying that my son is a problem for you. What you really mean is that you think my son is barking mad and therefore not safe to be left with the other kids.

Knowing that would be pointless to argue Gina simply stood up and left the headmistress's room. Harry was outside sat on a chair in the corridor waiting for her with his back pack.

—I am sorry Mum.

Gina didn't know what to say. She was too angry but didn't want to lose it with him so she decided not say anything.

—I was scared. I could see them. It was two men mum. The same men I saw the other times...

—Enough Harry. Let's go home

Hours later...

—It's so nice to see you Paul, said Gina whilst embraced at Paul outside her home.

—It's alright now, said Paul stroking her hair.

—I am sorry I couldn't come earlier. We had only received the footage from our correspondent in Syria when you called me. It's horrifying what's happening in there right now.

—Sorry Paul for making you worried and taking you away from work...

—Don't worry sweetheart. It's alright. You were crying on the phone and I would never leave you crying. I might have to go back to work later to approve the final editing though. Let me take you for a dinner.

—Are you sure you can leave work now with so much going on?

—Yeah. It's completely fine. Juliana is looking after the kids isn't she?

—Yes she is – said Gina looking very sad.

100

—Ok then. So let's go to your favourite Italian in Richmond. I am sure that will help to cheer you up.

Gina went inside to say goodbye to the kids and did ask Juliana to put them into bed.

Gina told Paul about the incident earlier in school whilst they were on their way to the restaurant. When they arrived they were welcomed by the owner, Angelo.

—Ciao Paul, Ciao Gina. What a nice surprise to see you here — said the man with a very strong Italian accent.

—Ciao Angelo — said Paul and Gina almost at the same time.

—How are you two doing? I haven't seen you two for quite a while.

—We are fine thanks — responded Paul

—How's the kids Gina? — asked Angelo with a very strong Italian accent.

—They are all fine Angelo...well you know, cheeky as usual though they are all fine.

—I have your favourite table available. Please take a seat.

—Thanks Angelo - said Paul.

—Bear with me and I will bring your focaccia with the sardella that you guys like and of course...the wine!

They both sat and after few minutes Angelo served them with their favourite starters and wine. Angelo was originally from Naples and had known Paul for many years. He was a very enthusiastic and endearing guy and perhaps because of his advanced age and his father figure Paul had a lot of care for him. Since Paul introduced Gina and the kids to him she had also fell enchanted for Angelo and his restaurant had become the couple's favourite. At Angelo's they were not only served with traditional Italian food though it was also a place they knew they could recharge their energies. Angelo had a contagious passion for life. He was very loud and vibrant. His positive energy was highly contagious making everyone around him to feel comfortable and happy.

—I still feel awful. And even though I know he is not guilty I couldn't even look at him this time.

—Gina, it's not his fault. We need to find out what's happening to him.

—The doctors said that there's nothing wrong with him. The psychologist said that it's because of Michael's death. She took a long breath and continued. But now he has been expelled from school!

—I wouldn't worry about the school. This is a minor issue. We will be fine finding another school. Let's focus now on how we are going to help him.

—It pains me to remember his sad eyes today though I just couldn't speak to him.

—Don't blame yourself sweetheart. You also need time. It's been very hard for you. Why don't you try...

—What? You're not also thinking of...

—Yes, the spiritual centre Isabel and Juliana have been inviting you to go.

—Oh Paul, not you. I already have Juliana and Isabel banging on this idea and now you!

—What have you got to lose? We have taken Harry to so many doctors and specialists and no one has helped him. He keeps on saying that those men in black are after him and he says he feels scared. I don't know Gina... but maybe we could try it.

Suddenly Gina opened a shy smile.

—Why are you smiling for?

—I have only realised...

—What? asked Paul curious.

—I only realised that you have been saying we instead of you or I.

—Yes...I have. Haven't I?

Paul held her hands and looked firmly into her eyes and said;

—I love you Gina. I loved you since Michael first introduced me to you all those years ago. I wouldn't say anything; I would never betray my cousin and best friend even though at times my feelings for you were so

102

strong. I can't explain why though I don't think we have to explain love. I simply Love you and want to share my life with you.

Gina went silent for a while and after few seconds she dried a tear that ran down her face and said;

—In the beginning I didn't know if I was feeling like this for you because I was vulnerable or perhaps if because I felt safe next you...At times I felt guilty because I thought that perhaps I was betraying Michael though...the truth is that I didn't feel the happiness I feel when I am with you whilst I was with Michael. With you I feel safe, I feel loved though at the same time I feel a sort of freedom I didn't experience with him. Please don't take me wrong. I love him though somehow with you things feel more special in a way that it never felt before. Michael could be very jealous and possessive and only now I realise how much of my own life, my own wishes and personal projects I ended up leaving behind in order to be with him. I loved Michael though only now I understand perhaps I should have been stronger and not putting myself in second place as I did.

Gina shed a tear and after a brief pause she continued;

—With you it feels like everything flows so easy. Feels like if we have been together for a life time. I love you Paul.

Chapter XII
Liverpool 1826

Felicity was at home knitting when the front door opened and closed, making a loud noise. It was Peter, who had come back home in the middle of the afternoon and had rushed upstairs to the bedroom. Felicity went after him to try to find out what had happened. When she reached the bedroom she found Peter getting undressed. His clothes were on the floor, covered in blood. Felicity screamed in horror.

—I killed that black, Peter was saying, talking to himself. I killed that bastard!

Felicity was petrified in the corner of the room. Peter, who seemed to be out of breath, carried on talking.

—I had to do it. The bastard killed my father.

Felicity could not believe what she was seeing.

—Mr Worley is dead? Who did that to him? What are you talking about?

Peter was rushing to put on fresh new clothes.

—They caught my father in a trap, he replied. My father was killed by their leader. Luckily my intuition told me that something bad was happening, so I went to meet my father and took some of my fellows with me. When I got there I found the cowards. Their leader was stabbing my father in the back. My father didn't even have a chance to defend himself. I ran after them, and while my fellows got the others, I got the coward and stabbed him right through his heart. He will never defy a white man again.

Felicity was horrified while listening to her husband. She went down to the floor to collect her husband's dirty clothes, speechless.

Finally Peter was dressed again.

—There are lots of them out there who are now longing for revenge, he said, and I need to leave town for a while. I want you to be safe, so I am leaving one of my men here to watch out for you. He will be in charge of your security.

—Where are you thinking of going? And what about the factory and all the businesses?

—I have people whom I trust looking after my father's businesses and also the factory. I'll be in touch.

And without saying anything else he left the house. Felicity sat down on the end of the bed, holding his dirty clothes, staring into space.

Miranda came into the bedroom and asked her what had happened. Felicity told her.

—And he left without saying where he is going or when he is coming back, she said.

—You are better without him, my darling, and you know that. You have been having such a hard time with that man. Now you can have some free time. Since you got married you haven't been able to leave the house on your own or even see your friends. You have been a recluse in this house for more than four years now. You were so positive and vibrant, and now that man has brushed away all your shine.

Felicity remained quiet and pensive while Miranda was talking to her.

—Don't be scared, my dear, I am always here to look after you, said Miranda, finally getting a smile back from Felicity.

—Thanks, Miranda. You have been an angel in my life. I know you're right; this time will be good for me. I am just too scared of being on my own. At the end of the day I am not as strong as you think I am. But thanks for always being there for me.

Weeks passed by with no sign of Peter returning, and although there was always the threat of being attacked by someone who wanted revenge on Peter, Felicity seemed to enjoy the time without her husband being around. All the pressure, the arguments and the jealousy of Peter had vanished, and she was getting her life and her glow back.

One day whilst having breakfast she mentioned to Miranda that she was curious about the work they did at the local orphanage. She had heard amazing things about the work a lady and her son were doing, and asked Miranda to accompany her to pay them a visit. Miranda loved the idea and agreed to go with her after lunch.

Later that day the two ladies and one of Felicity's minders went over to the orphanage.

When they knocked on the door they were greeted by Beatrice, who had a friendly face.

—Hello, how can I help you?

—Hi, Madame, let me introduce myself. I am...

Felicity was interrupted by Miranda.

—This is my lady Miss Brown, Miranda lied, and I am her minder Miranda. We heard so many good things about your home and we thought we would pay a visit and learn more about your fabulous work.

Felicity didn't understand why Miranda had lied, but she smiled at Beatrice.

—Yes, she said. We would like to get to know more about the work you do and maybe even offer some extra help.

Beatrice welcomed them in. The two ladies went inside, leaving the minder outside.

Beatrice started by showing Felicity and Miranda the children's dormitories. She explained that due to their financial limitations and also a lack of space, they could only look after twenty kids. She showed them the kitchen and the dining room, which had a table long enough for twenty or more to sit down and have a meal together. Finally she showed them the classrooms.

—This is the room the children like the most. The arts and music room. My son Jonathan is teaching them music – until we can find a music teacher.

When Beatrice opened the door to introduce her guests to the children and her son, the kids ran from their desks towards her and all of them screamed with happiness. They surrounded Beatrice, trying to give her a hug. And it was there in the middle of that confusion, with all the kids making a lot of noise, and surrounding them with lots of energy, that Felicity and Jonathan met for the first time. Their eyes met and they seemed to be at that moment far away from all of that confusion.

Beatrice introduced them.

—Miss Brown and Miranda, I would like to introduce you to my son, Jonathan. He is a doctor and he also teaches the children English, maths and some other studies. Son, this is Miss Brown and her minder, Miranda. They came to visit us and learn more about our home.

Jonathan smiled, his eyes fixed on Felicity.

—It's a pleasure to meet you, ladies.

Noticing that all the children were impatient and trying to get some attention, Jonathan ordered them to calm down.

—Come on, children, let's all sit down! Ladies – please pull up a chair and take a seat. We will sing you a song. OK, children – I want you to show to our two visitors the song you know.

All the kids screamed in agreement.

—OK. When I say three, let's all sing the *Birds Flying High in the Sky* song.

Once again the kids shouted, saying yes, and Jonathan then counted.

—One ... two ... three ...

The children sang the song, accompanied by Jonathan. Felicity was watching everything and admiring Jonathan's natural way with the children. The three ladies clapped their hands along with the song. Miranda looked at Felicity throughout the song and noticed Felicity smiling. That was the first time she had seen Felicity smiling and happy for a long time. Jonathan went to the piano and he and the children played and sang another five songs. The atmosphere in the room was of a lot of happiness and joy. Felicity could feel, for the first time in her life, bliss – a special feeling that she had never had the chance to experience before.

After the songs, Beatrice invited Miranda and Felicity to go down to the living room for a cup of tea. Miranda and Beatrice left first, leaving Felicity alone with Jonathan and the kids. They were both enchanted with each other.

Felicity broke the silence.

—Thank you for this. It was so beautiful and so special. It was truly magical.

—No need to say thanks. It was our pleasure. And anyway, they love showing off their new tricks.

—I'd better be going, said Felicity with a shy look.

—I hope to see you soon, Miss Brown.

Felicity left the room, and when she closed the door she could feel that her heart was beating faster than usual. She felt different, as if she had butterflies in her stomach.

Beatrice was always very excited when talking about the orphanage and her work. In the living room she explained the work they did with the kids, and she also spoke about her son. Her passion for the work was contagious and inspiring. Felicity and Miranda were completely focused on every word Beatrice was saying. Beatrice introduced them to the rest of the staff in the house. Before leaving, Felicity plucked up the courage and, despite feeling shy still, asked Beatrice a question.

—I remember you said earlier that you are waiting for a music teacher. Do you have anyone in mind? I mean ... I have studied piano.

—We are always looking for extra help, my dear. We need someone who can teach the children piano or any kind of musical instrument, especially now that they are so motivated about learning more about music and the arts. Please join us.

—I would love to, replied Felicity smiling.

Miranda had also offered to help on whatever was needed, and they all agreed that Felicity and Miranda would start the following day, just after lunchtime.

The minder was still waiting for them outside the house. Felicity turned to Miranda.

—Why did you lie about my real name? I have never lied in my life before.

—Felicity, my dear, they would not have welcomed us in the same way if they knew that you are a Worley. Did you forget how hated your husband and his family are?

Noticing that this upset Felicity, Miranda changed the subject.

—I feel so good after visiting them – what a nice place. I can see you had a great time too.

—I know, agreed Felicity. I feel so good too. The love that they have for what they do and for the children. I almost cried when Beatrice was telling us about the horrible living conditions before they arrived at the orphanage.

—I know. I also felt sad for those poor little things. But now they look so happy and, more importantly, they look so healthy. By the way, her son is very handsome, Felicity. I saw the way he looked at you. His eyes were shining.

Felicity changed the subject, though she was feeling excited about coming back the following day and perhaps meeting Jonathan again.

That night at the orphanage, Beatrice and Jonathan were at the dinner table having their supper. The subject was their visitors earlier on in the day.

—So who are they, mother? What do they do?

—They said that the lady, Miss Brown, is the daughter of a captain who lives away from home most of the time, and that her mother died. She is bored at home and she heard about our work and wanted to come in and offer to help us. To be honest, son, I think I ended up by talking too much, as per usual, and not giving them much space.

Jonathan smiled at his mother.

—She was a very good-looking lady, he said, and she seemed to have a good way with the kids. Is she engaged?

Beatrice was surprised by Jonathan's interest, as she had never heard her son talking about a lady before. Jonathan had been very devoted to his studies, and now he was very devoted to her and his orphanage duties. Wanting to know more about her son's thoughts about Miss Brown, she carried on the subject.

—I am not sure, but she didn't mention any man's name. I guess you will be happy to know that she will be coming here more frequently from now on.

Jonathan's eyes widened.

—And why is this?

—Well, as it happens she has played the piano from an early age, and now she is going to be giving music lessons to our children.

—But I teach music to the children, said Jonathan.

Beatrice gave him a cheeky smile.

—Well, she said, it seems like you have a teaching partner for your music classes now. She starts tomorrow after lunch.

Later that night both Jonathan and Felicity in their different beds could not stop thinking about the meeting earlier. They both reviewed that first meeting second by second. They thought through every word and gesture of that brief meeting.

The following day Felicity tried on different outfits for her work at the orphanage. She had been feeling butterflies in her stomach for the entire night and that morning too. Miranda was feeling so happy for Felicity that she was enjoying just watching Felicity running around the house, trying on different dresses and singing like a teenager who had fallen in love for the first time. Miranda also appreciated how important it was for Felicity, who was feeling free from the oppressive life she had endured with Peter.

After lunch they were both ready outside the door of the orphanage.

—You look gorgeous, Miss Brown, said Miranda fixing Felicity's hat.

Felicity giggled after Miranda's comment and showed her shaky hands to Miranda to show her how excited she was. They knocked on the door and the door opened and they were once again greeted by Beatrice, who gave them both a warm hug and welcomed them in.

—Hello, both of you, nice to see you again, said Beatrice offering them a cup of tea.

—No, but thanks for asking – we are here looking forward to starting our work, said Felicity with a shyness about her.

—Oh yes, of course, said Beatrice smiling. I'll take you upstairs. The children have just finished their lunch and they are all upstairs waiting for their music class.

The three ladies went upstairs to the arts room. When Beatrice opened the door, to Felicity's disappointment Jonathan wasn't there. The kids were being minded by one of the staff members, Teresa. They were all sitting on their chairs and drawing.

—I have to apologise, Miss Brown. My son had a last-minute appointment, so you are going to do the class on your own. I hope you'll be alright. I will ask Teresa to stay and help you in case you need her, as they can be a bit naughty sometimes.

Felicity smiled, and even though she felt disappointed that Jonathan was not there, she was looking forward to spending time with the children and playing the piano for them.

Beatrice announced to the children that Felicity would be teaching them music and asked them to be respectful to their new teacher. Beatrice and Miranda then left the room, leaving Felicity with Teresa and the children.

It took Felicity a while to calm the children down, but once she started to play the piano the room fell silent and they all paid attention to her song. After playing the first song she invited the children to join her around the piano and taught them a new song that they could sing along to while she played the piano. They sang for over half an hour. The room was full of joy and laughter. The children seemed to enjoy Felicity's company, but most of all Felicity seemed happier than ever. At one point she had two little girls sitting on her lap, and the others were around the piano, some smiling and some giggling. Suddenly they heard the tall wooden door open, and to Felicity's delight it was Jonathan, who had just got back.

—May I come in and join you all?

—Yes! screamed the children at once.

—Please sing me one of the new songs you have just learnt with your new teacher.

—Come on, boys and girls, said Felicity with a shine in her eyes. Let's sing the song *Home! Sweet Home!* once again. Let's show Mr Jonathan what a beautiful song you have just learnt.

She counted to three and they all started to sing.

Jonathan was watching with amusement the natural way that Felicity had with the children and at the same time he was also admiring her beauty. Felicity had a glow in her face; her eyes were shining and her smile was contagious. Jonathan was completely enchanted by Felicity. They finished singing the song and Jonathan was still focusing on Felicity, who still had the two little girls on her lap. Jonathan blushed when he realised he had been caught staring at Felicity. The door opened again and Beatrice entered the room.

—Hi, son – I see you're back.

—Hi, mother. I got here literally a few minutes ago and they have just finished singing a song for me. Miss Brown has done a brilliant job.

—OK children, said Beatrice in a high tone of voice. It's time now for a small break. I'll take you all to the refectory where you will try a delicious cookie and a yummy cake that has been baked by our new friend, Miss Miranda. Come on, now, go in line.

The kids ran towards Beatrice and made a line going from the smallest at the front to the tallest at the end of the line. Beatrice headed to the refectory followed by the children.

—Congratulations, Miss Brown, said Jonathan. You tamed them and I can tell you that isn't an easy job.

—Oh no, they were great, she replied. As soon as I started playing the piano they listened to me and paid attention, and after the first song I began to teach them the song's lyrics so they could sing along while I played.

—I could see that they really like your company and that's something special. Kids are very perceptive and they can read people very well. If they like you and welcomed you so easily, like they did, it must be because you're a very special lady.

Felicity blushed and smiled, not saying anything back. They had a silent moment where they kept on looking into each other's eyes, until they were interrupted by Miranda.

—Excuse me Miss Brown, and Jonathan. I am here only to say that it's time for us to leave. I am sorry, Felicity, but we have to go.

Felicity knew Miranda very well and knew that something was wrong, and so she didn't hesitate.

—I am sorry but we have to go, said Felicity with a sad face.

—That's a shame, said Jonathan. I guess I'll see you tomorrow for another class?

—Yes, I'll be here after lunch.

—And I won't arrange any other appointments so that I can see you tomorrow, Miss Brown.

Felicity and Miranda left the orphanage and as usual the minder was waiting for them outside the house. As soon as they were outside Felicity asked Miranda what had happened and why they needed to leave so quickly.

—I had one of those feelings, you know.

—Your intuitions, Miranda?

—No, this time it was a vision. I saw your husband – he is about to come back home. I don't know when. I got so worried about you that I thought it would be better to go back to the house and try to find out what's happening. I don't want to even think of what that man would do to you if he found out that you have been working at the orphanage.

Felicity nodded towards the minder and whispered to Miranda.

—Do you think this man would tell my husband about our visits to the orphanage?

—We should never trust anyone linked with your husband, Miranda whispered back.

Once they got back to their house they found Peter in the living room, walking impatiently in circles around the room.

—Where have you been? I've been worried about you, said Peter grabbing Felicity by the arm.

—I've been to the market with Miranda. I couldn't bear staying at home anymore, so I needed some fresh air.

—You didn't buy anything at the market?

—We only went for a walk and to get some fresh air ...

He shook Felicity and looked at the man who had been minding her.

—Is that true?

Felicity had gone pale. She looked into her minder's eyes as if pleading with him to confirm her lie.

The man paused before replying to Peter's question.

—Yes, sir. I have been watching your wife and today was the first time that she went out. I escorted her and her servant to the market and I can guarantee they didn't speak to anyone.

Peter let Felicity go and pointed a handgun at the man, threatening him.

—You know that I will kill you if I find out that you're lying to me?

—Yes, sir. What I said is the truth.

—OK, you can leave now, Peter said to the man.

He then screamed at Miranda to leave too.

Peter seemed to have aged years in the few months that he had been away. He had a long beard and rough skin.

—Now I want to remember my wife, he said to Felicity. Let's go to the bedroom.

Felicity had learnt that it was better not to resist than to make her husband even angrier. She followed her husband and cried as she climbed the stairs.

The following morning, once Peter had left the house to do his business, Miranda rushed to the bedroom to see Felicity. She found Felicity still in bed, pale and looking depressed. Miranda held her for a long time before Felicity broke the silence.

—I felt so happy in that place, I felt like I could be free. And now I am a prisoner again. I had a feeling that my husband would never come back.

—You don't have to stop going to the orphanage, said Miranda.

—What do you mean? He is back. He would kill me and you if he found out we have been there.

—Well, we can find a way for you to leave the house without your husband knowing that you have left. You know that he goes out in the morning, comes back for lunch, and then goes out again, only returning late in the evening. That should be time enough for Miss Brown to go down to the orphanage and return before he comes back.

Felicity stood up quickly, feeling happy about the suggestion and the possibility of going back to the orphanage. Miranda and Felicity began to analyse all the options she had in order to execute the plan. She visited the orphanage that afternoon and did so for months without telling her husband. Soon after Peter had left the house after his lunch she would leave the house using the back yard door, so none of her husband's men could see her leaving, and she would then spend the afternoon in the company of Beatrice, the children and Jonathan. Those hours in the afternoon were the only time in her whole life that she could relax and find peace. At the orphanage she could be herself and there she found love for the first time. Jonathan and Felicity had fallen in love with each other the first time they met. Although they had never spoken to each other about their feelings towards each other, they both enjoyed the short hours they spent in the afternoon surrounded by the children, and their love grew stronger and stronger. Felicity had never revealed her true identity to Jonathan, fearing that he would hate her for being a Worley, and although he found it strange that Felicity was so secretive about her life, the love he felt for her was so strong that he could not hold any bad thoughts towards her.

Deep down Felicity knew that one day she would be caught by Peter, as she knew that it didn't matter how long the truth had been buried in the ground – it would always come up and reveal itself.

Although she knew that she was taking a big risk by defying her husband, she felt a massive feeling of strength after she had fallen in love for the first time. For Felicity the risk she was taking in order to see the love of her life was worth it.

The picture faded away and Michael was then back to the room where Gabrielle and Nina were sleeping.

Michael was shedding tears – tears of sorrow. He had remembered another important part of his previous life experience in Liverpool. He looked around the room where he was and immediately recognised it as being the bedroom where he had lived with Felicity. He could not stop the tears from coming down his face.

—This is the house ...

Michael cried out in anguish.

—Why am I back in this horrible place? Mother, I need you. Please help me!

Next to him Gabrielle was asleep with her mother on the same bed Oscar had passed away in the day before. Mother and daughter were holding each other. The entire room brightened up with the same light he had seen before. Juliana's mentor appeared in the room. She looked like a mature lady; she was black with African features. She got closer to Michael, who was lying down on the floor, still crying.

—Hello Michael.

Michael had his hands covering his face as if he was feeling embarrassed, as he was crying non-stop. The lady went down on her knees and touched his head with her right hand.

—My name is Regina. Don't feel embarrassed, Michael. We are all learning and sometimes we make mistakes. It's down to us to learn from our mistakes and use them to purify our spirits.

Regina dried his tears with her hands and continued.

—God always gives us the opportunity to start over again so we can repair the bad we have done. Look around you. It was your decision to leave the spiritual colony that brought you here. Make the most out of the present moment and use your energy and your time to help those around you.

Regina pointed to Gabrielle and her mother, who were sleeping in bed.

—I don't feel I can. I don't have any energy. All I have been doing for the past few days is lying down on this floor watching all the misery around me.

—Yes you can. Focus your thoughts and energy on positive things. Pray, pray to the Lord to give you strength.

—I am scared. The dark legion is after me. They are only waiting until they get hold of John Worley, who they think is my father. Once they got their hands on him they will then get revenge.

Michael was very frightened. The words were coming out of his mouth very fast, making it almost impossible to understand what he was trying to say.

—First of all, you are not chained, said Regina. The physical cannot work on the spiritual. What you have is an illusion. You have chosen to believe these spirits instead of believing in God above all. The chain you are imagining only exists in your mind and their minds. Once you recover your true faith in God you will free yourself from the suffering you have put yourself through. Second of all, the legion won't be able to kill your dad – not if it's not in God's will.

—What do I do? How do I get out of here?

—Remember there are consequences to all of our acts. You brought yourself to this situation. Now you can't deny help to Gabrielle and Nina. Stay here until the time to leave arrives. Until then you can send Gabrielle and Nina positive energy and heal their spirits. Pray with your heart and the prayer will brighten your spirit and illuminate those around you too.

—What about the legion? What if they come back?

—Pray with your heart. Talk to God and help will come!

—What about my mother and Mateo? How are they?

—They are fine. You could not see them but they have all been visiting you. Harriet has been praying for you. What the legion doesn't know is that God is everywhere. All this time you have been assisted by your spiritual guides and angels. Nothing happens without God's approval. If God allowed those inferior spirits to bring you here, it's because He wanted you here and not because those inferior spirits had the power to get you here.

Regina stood up and lifted Michael up. She looked straight into his eyes.

—Before I go, she said, I would like to give you a message. Harriet asked me to tell you that she knows you have recovered an important part of your past, and she wanted to say that you are soon to recover the rest of it. It will be very disturbing when that happens, but she wants to assure you that she will be with you when it does. When that happens you will then understand the whole truth of today's happenings.

Regina lifted both her arms, closed her eyes and prayed. At that moment the bright light in the room turned into a soft blue light. Michael felt very peaceful, as if his energy had been renewed.

—Goodbye Michael. Remember that the purer your thoughts become, the closer to God you will be.

Chapter XIII
The Chico Xavier Spiritual Home

—I still can't believe I've agreed to this, said Gina to Isabel in the car.

—You don't trust me, do you Gina? said Isabel laughing. You will change your mind, just you wait and see.

When they arrived at the spiritual home they met Juliana, who was waiting for them outside.

—So this is it? asked Gina.

Juliana laughed.

—I guess you didn't expect it to be this 'normal', did you? she said.

—I am just surprised, because to me it looks like a normal house in North London.

—This is the house Amelia converted to use as a spiritual home, Isabel explained. Before it used to be one of her properties and she used to rent it out. She opened the spiritual home after her teenage son passed away. A few months after his passage she saw his spirit, who appeared to her and asked her to study Allan Kardec's doctrine and the spiritual world. He also asked her to use some of the family's wealth and engage in charity work to help the poor. Her son advised her to visit a spiritual home in a small town in the countryside of Brazil, where Chico Xavier used to deliver messages from disincarnated spirits to their families. After meeting Chico Xavier, Amelia was so touched and inspired that on her return she opened this spiritual home and named it after him. Amelia comes from a very wealthy family, and because of her son's request Amelia is engaged with several different charities. One of them, which is run from this centre, is to help a group of homeless people. The group receive a healthy meal every week which is cooked by volunteers, and they also receive working classes to enable them to reintegrate into the community. We have teachers who volunteer and give their time once a week to teach them ...

—Come on guys, Juliana interrupted. The meeting will start soon – let's go in. Come on kids.

It was a very spacious house. Inside there was a room large enough to hold a hundred people or more. The room had white walls with a few pictures on and one portrait of Jesus Christ in the centre of one of the walls. People were gathering in the main entry room, most of them drinking healed water or tea. Juliana and Isabel showed Gina the second room where the actual meetings took place. The second room was as big as the entry hall and had a very long table with over thirty chairs around it. There were French doors at the end of the room leading out to a very green garden.

—What about the picture of Jesus on the wall? I thought it was a spiritual place, said Gina while trying to get Kit and Grace together.

—And Jesus isn't a spirit like you and me? He is the purest spirit and we aim to follow his steps and teachings. All of Allan Kardec's work is based on the Gospel and follows Jesus' teachings.

Juliana went on to explain to Gina that her job was to look after the children in a separate room where they taught the gospel according to spiritism through games and activities. She took Gina and the kids upstairs where they found several rooms. They walked into a room where kids were gathering.

—This is the children's room. Here we teach them basic

knowledge of the doctrine such as to respect others, to love one another, and very basic lessons from the gospel. At the same time our mentors in the spiritual world are here working, healing the children and treating those who need any support. If any of the children are being tormented by an inferior spirit, the tormenting spirit and the child are treated in the healing sessions. This is the section I work in once a week. Every week I help the other volunteers to look after the children and teach them the gospel according to spiritism.

Juliana gestured towards Kit and Grace.

—Leave them with me and I will look after them whilst you attend the meeting downstairs.

Gina knew that she could trust Juliana, and Kit and Grace were soon enchanted with the new toys they found around the room and mixed very quickly with the other kids. Harry seemed a little hesitant and reluctant to stay there, but he liked Juliana and stayed under the condition that she held hands with him the whole time.

Downstairs in the main meeting room everybody was now sitting around the long rectangular table. Gina sat on the only empty seat, next to Isabel.

—What do I need to do? whispered Gina to Isabel.

—Nothing, just be quiet now! The meeting is about to start.

Amelia, who was sitting at the centre of the table, spoke in a very soft tone of voice.

—I want to welcome you to this home of peace and light. I know we have some new friends here and I wanted to say a special welcome to you and say that the only requirement in this home is that we are all in a positive vibration. So please empty your mind, letting all the bad thoughts go. It's time to refresh our thoughts and renew our souls. Let all the old and bad thoughts out in order to free our souls and feed them with new and peaceful energy.

Amelia continued and invited everyone to do an initial prayer to open the meeting.

—Our Lord, all-powerful God, please allow the good and superior spirits to be present and guide us during our meeting. Fill this home with your knowledge and take us away from thoughts of selfishness, jealousy, anger and envy. May all the support be present to help those who are in need of help and guidance, and may all the maleficent spirits be taken away to learn about love and the true meanings of life. Friends of the spiritual world who were sent by God almighty to protect mankind, we invite you to our meeting to bring peace to those who are in despair and feeling lost, to bring love and happiness to those who are in involved in dark thoughts, and to guide all of us towards God's greatness.

Around the table they all had their eyes closed. Whilst Amelia and the attendees prayed, Mateo and other spirits of light were going around the room, touching every single attendee's head and praying for each individual. After finishing the prayer, Amelia invited everyone to discuss a passage of the Gospel that says *Return good for evil; love your enemies.*

—Matthew, 5:43–47. Ye have heard that it hath been said, thou shalt love thy neighbour, and hate thine enemy. But I say unto you, love your enemies, bless them that curse you, do good to them that hate you, and pray for them which despitefully use you, and persecute you; that ye may be the children of your Father which is in Heaven: for He maketh his sun to rise on the evil and on the good, and sendeth rain on the just and on the unjust. For if ye love them which love you, what reward have ye? Do not even the publicans do the same? And if ye salute your brethren only, what do ye more than others? Do not even the publicans so?

Amelia continued reading The Gospel According to Spiritism by Allan Kardec.

—'When he spoke, Jesus did not mean that each one of us should have the same tenderness for an enemy as would be felt for a brother, sister or a friend. Tenderness presupposes confidence; well, no one can deposit confidence in another person knowing that they bear malice. No one can show effusive friendship knowing that the other person is likely to abuse the situation. Between people who have no confidence amongst themselves there cannot be the same manifestations of sympathy that exist between those who share the same ideas. Therefore, to love one's enemy doesn't mean to show affection which would not be within our nature. To love one's enemy means we should not hate, not bear rancour against them, not desire vengeance. It means to forgive all the evil they have caused without any hidden thoughts or without any conditions. It means to wish them well instead of bad things. It's to have joy instead of regret, at the good things that may come their way. Whosoever can proceed this manner fulfils the conditions of the commandment; Love one's evil.' Let's reflect on this passage of the gospel and discuss it. Why do we forgive our enemies and those who don't wish us well?

Whilst Amelia and the attendees were discussing what they had just read, Mateo and the other spirits of light were attending to disincarnated spirits who had been brought to the centre with the desire of finding help and support.

—Tell me my brother, asked Mateo, what made you come here?

The spirit, who had the form of a young guy, answered him.

—I have been told by a lady to come here and see you. I died years ago, and at first it was quite difficult for me to accept my situation. I thought it was unfair for an eighteen-year-old, with so much ahead of

125

him, to die. I was then visited by my grandparents, who explained more about my new condition, and they have been inviting me to go and live with them at the same colony. I want to accept my grandparents' invitation, but I feel like I should not leave my parents' house. My parents cry every single day, especially my mum, and I feel that if I leave I will cause them to suffer even more.

—First of all, son, you are not dead; otherwise you would not be talking to me right now, right? You have ended your life experience here on the earth, and now it's time for your mother and father to understand you live on but not in your material human body. You need to depart so you can continue to evolve, and they have to learn that they need to set you free. If you continue to deny your new condition as a spirit, you will get stuck in time and miss so many opportunities to continue developing your spirit.

—I want to go with my grandparents, but I feel so sorry for my parents.

—Trust God, son. Your parents will be guided. It's also part of their own learning to go through the loss. Sometimes we need to learn to let go, especially those we love, if it is for our own good. As you know your mother has been guided to this spiritual home this evening by the same spirit who guided you here. Your father still has his eyes closed to life after death, as he likes to call it, and unfortunately he didn't come. Please wait here and soon you will have the opportunity to communicate with your mother.

The next in line to be consulted was a young lady who had disincarnated exactly one year ago. Mateo consulted her and continued to serve the other spirits who were waiting for support and guidance.

Before the meeting came to an end, Amelia made an announcement.

126

—Friends of this spiritual home: our spiritual friends have been doing consultations with the spiritual visitors, and I have two messages for two of our friends present here tonight.

Amelia sat on the chair and closed her eyes. Mateo first brought in the boy next to Amelia. Holding his hand Mateo gave him a sign to start. Amelia repeated word by word what the boy said.

—Dear mother, it is with such pleasure that I see you visiting this home of peace and light. I have been watching you and dad at home and it pains me to see you crying and suffering over my passage day in and day out. Granddad John and Grandma Edna are inviting me to go and continue my life in the same spiritual colony as them. I have resisted all this time, but I feel that your suffering and mine are delaying our evolution and progress. We are all stuck in bad feelings, and so you two need to continue, as do I. Please remember me with love and joy and I assure you that one day we will all be together again. For now please let me go, as our sorrow isn't bringing any good to any of us. I love you and dad forever. Much love, Daniel.

The woman sitting next to Gina started to cry out loud.

—It's my son. It's my little boy! Oh, how I miss him.

Gina stood up and gave the woman a hug, giving her some comfort. After the woman calmed down, Amelia continued with a second message.

—Dear mum and dad. One year has passed since the fatal accident. I am here to explain to you and my beloved sisters that I have not chosen to quit my life. I didn't commit suicide. I know that for all this time you have been nurturing bad feelings, imagining I didn't love my life anymore, to the point of ending it. But please believe me it was an accident. I had stepped on the stool next to the window so I could reach the lock on the window, which had got stuck, but as my experience on

127

the earth had come to an end the divine blow was used at that moment to undo the bonds that linked my spirit to my human body. It was my time to return to the spiritual world. I would also like to let you know that I didn't feel any pain when I fell. Immediately my soul was taken to a recovery hospital in the spiritual world where my grandparents were waiting for me. Stop torturing your souls by feeling guilt, imagining you could have changed the facts, because you couldn't. You are excellent parents and I keep in my heart all the beautiful moments we spent together. I love you mum, dad, Lydia and Katie, and one day we will all reunite again. In the meantime I send you my love and prayers, hoping you find comfort. Much love from your daughter, Suzie.

A couple who were sitting opposite Gina hugged each other and cried. The woman looked relieved.

—Our Suzie, she said to her husband. She didn't ... She didn't commit suicide.

—I knew it, my love, that she wouldn't have done such a thing, replied the husband.

They held hands while tears fell down their faces. They were tears of relief for both parents, who had been through a difficult time imagining their daughter had ended her life by jumping out of the window.

Amelia opened her eyes and continued.

—Friends from the spiritual world, please enable us to find comfort for our problems and also help us to develop our souls.

She said a final prayer accompanied by some of the regular attendees and closed the meeting with the words, Let's all have a peaceful week.

At the end of the meeting, when all the adults were socialising in the main room, Amelia came over to speak to Isabel and meet Gina.

—Nice to meet you, Gina. I hope you have enjoyed our session this evening.

—I am still a little bit confused about everything, although I have to confess I was touched by the messages earlier, and I am happy I have finally come.

—It's normal to feel confused, especially if you still don't believe that we are all spirits searching for our evolution in the universe and that this world that we live in is only an opportunity that we have to have experiences and develop our souls. When we incarnate to live an experience in the material world, it's as if a veil has been thrown over our past. It's like God is giving us a new fresh start to make it right this time without having any impressions from the past.

—Juliana and Isabel were telling me about the charity work you do here and also in Brazil and about your commitment to the spiritism doctrine.

—Yes. One of the most important fundaments of our doctrine is charity. I don't know if they told you but when my teenage son, Rob, passed away, I had the privilege to receive a visit from him. His spirit came and talked to me. I guess I have always had the mediumship gift, but it was then that I realised that my channel with the spiritual world had been opened. I did more research about the doctrine and have been studying ever since.

—Is there any book you could recommend for a beginner like me?

—Yes, there are a few. Why don't you give me a call so we can arrange to meet for tea? We can have a cup of tea and talk through some good books and I can also explain a few things to you. Isabel, you are also invited. Let's arrange it for an afternoon next week, perhaps.

They all agreed to meet the following week. Amelia said she

would wait for a confirmation call from Isabel and they all said their goodbyes.

In the car on the way back, the kids were asleep peacefully on the back seat and Gina couldn't talk about anything else but her experience at the spiritual centre.

—I am still touched by those messages.

—I know, said Isabel. I am touched too. Every week there's usually a message for someone in the group. It's as if some spirits guide the visitors to come to the spiritual centre on the day, knowing that a message will be delivered. For example, the lady who came with her friend, the one who received a message about her son, told me that her friend was insisting she come for a long time, but as her husband never believed in such a thing she felt she shouldn't. She then mentioned that today she felt different, as if something was telling her to accept the invite. It ended up that her husband was out for a business dinner, and she decided to come with her friend. In my experience it's clear that she has been inspired by a friendly spirit to come in tonight, and perhaps the same happened to the spirit of her son who was guided to come in tonight and receive treatment.

—Maybe I could receive a message from Michael one day.

—Yes, I don't see why not, although a message is only delivered if it is going to be beneficial for both the one who is receiving and the one who's sending it.

The conversation continued for the entire journey. Isabel dropped Gina and the children home with the promise that she would ring Amelia and arrange the meeting for the following week.

Later on that night Gina felt totally relaxed, and although she was still reluctant to believe, the evening had helped her to be calmer and to stop having bad thoughts about Michael. Also, Harry seemed to

130

be different on the way home. He seemed calmer and he also had a more serene expression. She started to think about Harry and how different he was from the other two kids. How could he be so different from Grace and Kit? They all had the same education and were all raised in the same way. Paul came up in her mind and she suddenly started to feel well again. They had such good chemistry, and he also made her feel safe and secure, as if together they could find the solutions for any problem. The relationship with him was easy. It had a natural flow. No games, no discussions – very different from her relationship with Michael ... Gina fell asleep.

Chapter XIV
Harriet's Message

One week later ...

Gina left the kids with Juliana at home and went to visit Amelia with Isabel.

—Welcome, ladies. It's nice to have you here, said Amelia.

—Thanks for inviting us, replied Gina.

Amelia asked them to make themselves comfortable in the living room. She had prepared a full afternoon English tea with scones and cream, tea and cakes. Amelia finished decorating the table and serving the tea.

—I would like to start by saying that the biggest reason why I visited the spiritual home last week, admitted Gina, was because of my son Harry. He has been very angry and tormented since his father died, and I need to say a big thank you as his behaviour has completely changed. Before he was behaving aggressively towards everyone around him. But what was really scary was the fact that Harry kept on saying that he could see dead people. Men in black, as he used to call them.

Amelia was listening, paying a lot of attention whilst finishing decorating the table.

—I have tried psychiatrists and shrinks. He went through brain scans, but nothing abnormal showed up on his tests ... Well, the intriguing thing is that since we visited the spiritual home last week he seems to be back to how he used to be before Michael died. He is back to being that caring and loving boy he always used to be.

They all sat down to have their tea.

—Wow Amelia, the table looks amazing, said Isabel. You are always such a great hostess.

—Thanks Isabel. I'm happy to have you two here. And I am glad, Gina, to hear that our healing passes are working.

—I'm sorry – healing passes? What do you mean?

—It's like an energy healing session. Our spiritual guides send us vibrations of love and positivity. I need to say that in your son's case we still have to continue our work.

Amelia put her hands over Gina's hands as though trying to make her feel secure.

—Please don't be scared by what I am going to say now, as I guarantee there's always a solution. Your son has been tormented by some inferior spirits. Spirits who are very primitive and are desperate for vengeance.

—My son? But why is my little son going through such a horrible thing? He is only a child.

—We have all lived other lives and experiences before, and most of the troubles of the present life are the results or consequences of our actions from past lives. When talking about the spiritual world, forget about labels such as father, mother, friend, aunt, and think instead of all of us as being individuals who are here to learn in order to evolve and purify our souls. The spirit of your son is an individual like you and me and has its own learning to do and developments to make. At the sessions held at a spiritual home, both are treated: the incarnated spirits like you, me, Isabel, and your kids, and the spirits who are now in the spiritual world. When you came last week our spiritual guides who work with the children got to learn more about your son's history. They advised me that he is being tormented by primitive spirits, as I mentioned before. Those spirits insist on tormenting him.

—Oh my ... This sounds very scary indeed, said Gina.

—I am confident that everything will be fine. Our spiritual guides are working on educating and trying to help the spirits who are tormenting your son. I know for a fact that one of the spirits who are tormenting him is already changing its mind and turning to God, and it's only a matter of time before that spirit surrenders and goes to a learning spiritual colony. Your son is surrounded by beautiful souls like yourself, Paul and your other two kids, who are all willing to guide him on the path of love. There are also many elevated spiritual friends in the spiritual world who are helping by inspiring him with good thoughts and vibrations of peace.

—Can I help more? Is there anything more that I can do to help my son?

—Keep on showing Harry the beautiful things of life. Keep on leading by example and teaching him how to be a good human being. His main mission at this stage of his existence is to learn and practise kindness and respect to those around him. We can all help, but it will depend on your son to follow all those amazing examples of people he has around him and not fall into the traps of material life. Taking into consideration the progress we can see happening – and happening so quickly, too – I am confident he will be fine.

—Are these bad spirits going to go away and leave my son alone?

—They aren't bad, Gina, but actually very inferior in comparison to other spirits who don't carry feelings like anger and hate. They are spirits who don't know the meaning of love and forgiveness. As the message we studied in our meeting last week told us, we must learn to forgive our enemies. The more Harry progresses his soul, the less able to reach out for him those spirits will be. It's the same with all of us. The more we evolve our souls, the more pure we become. Surround yourself with love and love will surround you – this is what I say to my friends and dear ones all the time.

Mateo and Harriet were next to Amelia at that point. Holding hands, both felt happiness seeing Gina in the company of Amelia. They knew that they would be able to help Harry more now he was frequenting the spiritual home. They lifted their arms above the three ladies' heads and prayed, sending them vibrations of love. Harriet got closer to Amelia.

—My dear friend, he said, I have a communication I would like you to pass on to Gina.

—I am all yours, communicated Amelia with Harriet via thoughts.

Gina and Isabel noticed that Amelia had gone quiet for a moment. She had both hands over her face. After a few moments of silence, she repeated the words communicated to her by Harriet.

—*Gina, my dear, what a blessing it is to have had this opportunity from our superior guides to pass this message on to you. I wanted you to know that I have been watching out for you and the kids alongside other friends and we have all been inspiring you with thoughts of love and peace. I know you have been challenged with recent happenings with our Harry, and I would like to assure you that we are all watching out for you and helping to inspire and guide you all in these difficult times. Harry needs a lot of care and love and God entrusted him to the right family. You, Paul and the kids have all the love and knowledge Harry needs to follow and learn from in order to become a great man. If you ever find yourself troubled, with no answers, all you have to do is to channel your thoughts into love and God and pray, and I guarantee the answers and support will come to you. Mateo and I volunteer at the spiritual home, helping lost spirits who are in need of assistance and care, and we are very happy to see you and the kids being part of the same link of love. Send our love to Paul and invite him when you next visit. We will be delighted to see him frequenting the meetings. Much love, Harriet.*

—Such a touching message, said Isabel. Is she Michael's mother?

—Oh Harriet, said Gina, thinking of her mother-in-law and friend. Yes. She was Michael's mother. She was such a special woman.

She paused for a moment and then continued.

—I feel strange ... as if I can smell her fragrance in the air. Her presence feels so real, even though ...

Amelia interrupted Gina.

—She passed away, you mean? Stop thinking like that. Our life is infinite and our passage here on earth is just one of the many, many life experiences our spirits go through.

—What about Mateo? Who is he, Gina? asked Isabel.

—I don't know. As far as I remember Michael's father passed away when he was only a baby, though I don't remember his name being Mateo. Harriet never married again.

Gina took a long breath.

—Wow. I am speechless! she said.

—Mateo is a very moral and intellectual elevated spirit and he is our spiritual mentor and guide at the centre. He is the one who coordinates our spiritual works and the meetings at our spiritual home and ensures that our meetings flow well and that everyone receives the necessary assistance. Now, ladies, what if we hold our hands and pray to thank Harriet and thank our spiritual guides for the opportunity we have just had?

They prayed and thanked Harriet for her kind words and thanked Mateo and the spiritual guides for their protection and guidance. They continued their tea, talking about the message they had just received, and later on changed the subject and talked about the charity work done at the spiritual centre in London and the charity Amelia had in Brazil. Curious about the man Amelia had been to meet in Brazil, Gina asked her about Chico Xavier.

—I had the huge pleasure of meeting Chico one year before he returned to the spiritual world. His full name was Francisco Candido Xavier. I travelled there after receiving a message from my son. I hired a guide and translator who took me to a small town in Brazil called Uberaba where Chico lived.

—Tell me more about him, said Gina, as I have never heard of him before.

—Chico was a medium. He wrote over four hundred books and sold millions of copies. He never claimed to be the author of the books he wrote, as he used to say he was only the messenger for spirits. He used to psychograph the books. The royalties and profits from his work were always given away to charities and he led a very simple, dedicated life to help the people. He left us a legacy of novels, philosophy, romances and many works that teach us about love and the eternity of our spirits. As well as writing the books and raising money for the many charities he helped, Chico used to consult people who had travelled from different places to see him and receive a message from their loved ones who had passed away. For the days I was there I saw long queues of people lined up every day waiting to meet him. Chico would psychograph messages from spirits who wished to contact their families – very similar to the two messages we received last week, although they would always be written messages. He had such a peaceful energy around him. When I met him for the first time I burst into tears and I couldn't stop crying. They were not tears of sorrow. It was as if my spirit was crying with an immense blissful emotion. When he saw me for the first time he said that he was glad to see I had attended at my son's request to discover more about the doctrine. He also said that he knew about my intention of founding a spiritual home back in London and he was very happy about the idea. I spent four weeks serving the local poor families which his spiritual home helped, and for those four weeks I learnt so much from him.

—It sounds like he was an amazing man, said Gina.

—He was so inspiring. It was then that I realised I wanted to organise charity work in Brazil and in London. Chico used to say that there was no salvation without charity.

Gina and Isabel spent the rest of the afternoon talking and learning more about Amelia's experience back in Brazil and her charitable works.

Chapter XV
Michael's Return

—Stop crying, mother. Everything will be fine, said Gabrielle, drying the tears on Nina's face.

—You're so grown up for your age, said Nina. You are only seven. You deserve a better life.

—We both do, mother. We will find a solution, so please be strong.

—I don't feel I can. I am not strong. Sometimes I think the best thing is to give you away … Perhaps you would be better off if you were being raised by a different mother, someone strong.

Michael got closer to them both.

—You can do it, Nina, he said. You can stop drinking and raise your daughter. Look at her – look at the precious little girl you have. She loves you and she needs you. Fight for you and for her! You don't need a man to live your life. You have to do it for yourself.

Nina looked at Gabrielle.

—You think I am a bad mother, don't you?

—I don't think that, mum. I love you.

Gabrielle hugged her mother, and Nina hugged her daughter even tighter.

—You're so special, Gabrielle; you are so mature and smart. Sometimes you're the only reason I have for carrying on.

Slowly the quality of Nina's thoughts changed. When Michael

realised Nina had started to become more positive, he carried on sending her motivational thoughts. *You're a beautiful woman, Nina. Believe in yourself. Be strong, you can do it. Ditch the drink right now. Get yourself a job and occupy your mind with productive thoughts. You will see how life will take a turn for the better …*

—What are you doing, slave?

Michael was taken by surprise as he was pushed backwards by Buziba.

—Where is your chain, slave?

Enu pushed him aggressively. Both Enu and Buziba looked at Nina and Gabrielle and swore at them.

—Leave them alone, shouted Michael. Your problem is with me, not with them, so leave them alone! Your boss got Oscar and there's nothing here for you apart from me. I won't let you close to them ever again.

He was then grabbed by his throat and lifted up in the air. The entire room turned brighter with such intensity that the two dark legion followers were momentarily blinded. Mateo and Harriet arrived in the room, followed by Regina and some of Mateo's friends, who worked with him at Amelia's spiritual home.

—Enu, Buziba, leave him, said Mateo with authority in his voice.

They let Michael go and, looking very defiant, confronted Mateo.

—He is our slave, said Buziba. He needs to pay for what he has done. We will leave the two girls alone, but we won't give up this piece of nothing or let him and his father go free without paying for what they have done. We won't let the Worleys escape!

—Michael is untouchable, said Harriet. We are protecting him. You'd better give up.

Mateo addressed Enu.

—For how long are you going to delay your progress? Don't you feel tired of pursuing a path that is only holding you back? What have you achieved so far? There is so much more in the universe for you to discover and experience. Why do you keep on limiting yourselves to this? It's time to understand more about what you are and how many beautiful things you can achieve if you allow yourself to let go of these dark thoughts and this low energy. All the members of your family have moved on and they have all forgiven those who caused them pain. Why don't you do the same?

—You ain't gonna take us with you by using this cheap chat! said Buziba aggressively.

Regina now took the chance to speak to Enu.

—Enu, isn't it time for you to join your family? You used to use the excuse of revenge against those who had made you suffer, but what about all the suffering you have inflicted on other people? Were you not suffering the consequences of your own actions? God is giving you a chance to start again.

Regina held out her hand to Enu who accepted. Crying, he went down on his knees.

—Get up, Enu! said Buziba. What are you doing? You belong here with us! You are embarrassing me.

Regina embraced Enu and dried his tears. She turned to Buziba.

—You can take this opportunity and give yourself a new beginning, Buziba. I went through a life as a slave, as you did. I know the pain, but I have learnt to forgive. Your family has forgiven those who did bad things to them. Forgiving is our way to clear our spirits of bad feelings that can only delay our own progress. Forgive and move on, as we have.

—No way! I will never forget the cruelty of those white people who treated us with so much disrespect. They killed our people. They treated us as merchant goods, forgetting we were human beings. I will never forgive and I despise you for joining their company.

Buziba turned to Enu and told him that he was a traitor. Finally he pointed at Michael.

—You might be safe for now, Buziba said to him. But we will go after your son. We will get revenge on the Worleys! Your son will pay the price ...

Buziba left the room.

—Thanks all for your support and your good vibrations, said Mateo to his friends. Regina, my dear friend, please take Enu to a recovery centre where he can get himself treated until he is able to go to a colony. Harriet and I will stay and talk to Michael.

Everyone left the room apart from Harriet and Mateo. Harriet embraced Michael for a few moments.

—They won't bother you again, son, she said. As long as you keep your thoughts elevated and with vibrations of peace, the dark legion won't be able to get close to you again.

—It's been awful, Michael confessed. They made me their prisoner and it got to a point where I had no energy left.

—We have seen, Michael. Mateo and I paid frequent visits to you. There was not much we could do because you put yourself in that situation by lowering the quality of your thoughts, which lowered your energy to the same level as their energy. When your spirit engaged in dark thoughts, all you did was distance yourself from God, making your spirit accessible to inferior spirits.

—I thought God never let His children down?

—He doesn't. He never does. It was your choice. You distanced yourself. But we were always here watching out for you. All we could do was send you good thoughts and positive vibrations in the hope you would react and return to God, as you did in the end.

—Like Enu just did, said Mateo. Enu has been secretly praying and asking for forgiveness for a while and has finally returned home after centuries of living in the darkness. His brothers and sisters were also slaves, and when they disincarnated they chose to forgive their enemies. They chose to return home and use that experience as learning. Enu, on the other hand, chose revenge, anger. He didn't trust God's divine plans and thought he could enact justice, not knowing that he only could act whenever allowed by God, and even when he thought he was causing damage to someone all he was doing was being used as an instrument of God.

Harriet held Michael's hand.

—It's your time to return home now, she said. Come on, son. It's time to go.

Michael hesitated.

—That's what I want the most, but what about Gabrielle and Nina? I care a lot about them ... I could even say I feel love for them. I don't want to leave them now, when they are still so vulnerable.

Mateo put his hand on Michael's shoulder.

—They will be fine, he said. We will continue to visit them and send them vibrations of encouragement and love. Gabrielle is a very illuminated spirit – whom, by the way, you know from previous lives – and she has now incarnated to help Nina on her mission. We pray that Nina will keep strong and avoid the vices that have been her biggest enemy. An enemy that she chose herself.

Michael went up to Gabrielle and kissed her on the cheek.

—Keep on strong, little star, he said. You have been doing so well. I will come back to visit you. Goodbye for now, my little angel.

Michael, Harriet and Mateo held hands and left the room.

Chapter XVI
The Truth Never Dies

Michael, Harriet and Mateo were sitting around a table at Michael's house back at the Towers. They were all holding hands.

—It's a very sad moment of our lives, said Harriet. So I wanted you to know that it will be very difficult. Are you ready, Michael?

—Yes. I want to know the truth of what happened in that life experience in Liverpool.

—Let's close our eyes, said Harriet.

Mateo then said a prayer.

—Our Lord, God almighty, please allow us to revisit our past in order to learn and make a new beginning.

Liverpool ...

Peter was facing major financial problems at the textile factory and with the slave trade business that he had inherited from his father. He was getting home in the evenings stressed and more aggressive than usual. The hours he spent at work had increased over the past months, which meant that he was too busy to notice Felicity's visits to the orphanage. A few times he had come back home drunk and had been violent towards Felicity. She knew she couldn't fight him. At the beginning Felicity had given up her life and couldn't care if Peter had taken his own words seriously and killed her, but now things were different. She had found love and her whole life had been transformed.

The hours spent at the orphanage were Felicity's only time of happiness and peace. She adored her time with the kids, teaching them piano and singing. She knew every single child's personal history and felt very affectionate towards each and every one. They adored her too, and when gathering around the piano they would argue in order to get a chance to sit on her lap and receive a hug from their beloved teacher. Beatrice liked Felicity's company and she was feeling very happy for Jonathan, who seemed to be over the moon every time Felicity was in the house. Beatrice had also found a friend in Miranda, who accompanied Felicity on her visits.

Felicity and Jonathan fell in love with each other the first time they met. Every day after the classes they would hold hands and look straight into each other's eyes for minutes without even saying a thing, admiring each other's beauty and communicating their love only with looks.

Although Felicity felt very bad for lying to Jonathan and Beatrice about her true identity, she knew that was the only way she could keep on visiting the orphanage without being rejected by the two of them. Her husband and his family would understandably not have been welcome in their home. The longer the situation carried on, the more difficult she found it to tell the truth.

One day after the class, when the children had gone to the refectory for their afternoon tea break, Jonathan held Felicity's hand and looked into her eyes.

—I am afraid I can't help it anymore, he said. It's getting harder and harder …

—I don't understand, said Felicity even though her soul knew what he was about to say.

—You have brought sunshine to our home, Miss Brown, and every day gets harder. Harder because I am completely in love with you.

Felicity's heart rate accelerated. A rush of blood went though her body. She wanted to kiss him and tell him she had loved him since the first time she saw him. Even though she couldn't explain how it had happened, love was love, and it had happened for the first time in her life.

—Jonathan ... I ...

The lies she had been telling in order to be able to protect her fake identity came up in her mind. Suddenly the picture of Peter beating her came up too. That was her reality: a violent, possessive husband waiting for her at home. More and more thoughts came up until she exploded and let go of his hands.

—I have to go!

Felicity ran downstairs and left the house. Jonathan tried to follow her, but he was stopped by Miranda.

—Mr Jonathan, please don't. Let me go and find out what's happening.

Miranda apologised and left.

When Miranda reached home she found Felicity in tears.

—He loves me, Miranda. He loves me and there's nothing I can do. I am stuck with this man I don't love and there's nothing that I can do to change this.

Later that evening someone knocked on the front door while they were having dinner. Peter went to the front door to check what was happening. It was the factory supervisor.

—Sorry to bother you so late, Mr Worley. I thought I had to let you know that we have three kids who are very sick and unable to work.

—What do you mean they are unable to work?

—Our doctor said that we should reduce their working hours or they won't survive. All of our children are anaemic and suffering from malnutrition. We could lose our entire workforce if we carry on this way.

—Tell the doctor he won't tell me what to do in my factory. Those little devils are always giving us some kind of trouble. And I guess that you are probably being too gentle with them, and that's not why I pay your salary. Those children need a good lesson, I would say. Go back there and hit them hard as a punishment and threaten them, saying they will starve to death if they don't get a grip and get back to work.

—I am sorry, sir, but I am asking you to please come and check for yourself. They look very pale and they can hardly get up off the floor. I think the doctor is right – they are about to die.

—Go back there now and forget about this. Leave it with me and I'll sort those little bastards out tomorrow morning.

—Sir, the stock of soup for the children has come to an end and there's not much bread left. Would you have some food that I could take to the three sick children?

—Are you deaf or what? Didn't I say to forget about this? Leave it with me – I'll sort them out tomorrow morning. They are too lazy and I won't take this anymore. Go now.

The man left and when Peter got back upstairs he found Felicity at the top of the stairs facing him. She had listened to the conversation without him noticing.

—You're not leaving those three children to die are you?

—Who do you think you are to speak to me like this? I am not in the mood to explain myself to you right now. Go back to bed and go to sleep before I punish you!

147

—Peter, we've plenty of food here. They are only small children and they will probably die if you leave them without food for much longer. It isn't fair, the way you treat them …

Peter slapped her across the face.

—Don't ever call me Peter again. I am your husband!

Felicity didn't stop and for the first time she stood up to her husband.

—You need to help the children and stop mistreating them. You're not human but a monster!

—I've had a long day and I haven't got the energy to do this now, said Peter while pulling her hair as he tried to drag her to the bedroom.

Felicity pushed him with such strength that she managed to get rid of his hand. She tried to run away but she was grabbed by her neck. They fought violently until Felicity could not resist anymore and fell to the floor. She could not get back up. Her nose was bleeding and before she could move away, Peter pulled her by the hair and banged her head on the floor.

—Don't ever try to confront me again.

Miranda came into the room and when she saw Felicity bleeding on the floor, she screamed.

—Go back to your room, said Peter. I don't want you here! I've had enough of you blacks lately. You'd better leave before I hit you too.

—What did you do to her?

Miranda tried to get down on the floor where Felicity was, but she was pushed by Peter.

—Get out of here, I told you! he said.

Peter got hold of Miranda's throat and pressed her against the wall. He spat on her face and closed his right hand, getting ready to

148

punch her. Miranda closed her eyes. Before Peter could strike Miranda, Felicity hit his head with a crystal vase. Felicity and Miranda ran to the front door, but before they could leave Peter got hold of Miranda by her arm. He pulled a knife out of his pocket and stabbed Miranda. Surprised by his own action, Peter stepped backwards and walked way. Miranda was bleeding heavily. Felicity tried to hold her but Miranda removed the knife from her chest and stabbed Peter in the back. Peter fell face down on the floor followed by Miranda, who fell backwards.

—Go, Felicity, said Miranda. Get out of here. This is your chance. Go!

—I won't leave you here, Felicity replied. You're my family. I won't leave you here!

—Go, before this monster gets hold of you again. Run and ask for help. I am fine, Felicity. I am returning home. Don't worry about me.

—I love you, Miranda. You're my mother, my sister and my best friend.

—I love you too, my dear, but please, now, go, and get yourself away from this monster.

Felicity left the house, not knowing where to go.

The following morning, when Beatrice was going out to buy some bread, she found Felicity lying on her doorstep.

—My dear, what are you doing here? You have blood everywhere.

Beatrice rushed inside, shouting for help. Jonathan came to the door and found Felicity in his mother's arms, covered in blood. He checked her vital signs and made sure that she was OK. Felicity opened her eyes after a while, and when she realised that Jonathan and Beatrice were both looking worried and staring at her, she remembered what had happened the night before.

—Oh my God, how did I end up here?

—Calm down, my dear, said Beatrice. Stay calm.

—Try to stay calm, Jonathan told her, and to remember what happened. Mum, let's call a doctor.

—No, don't call the doctor. I am fine ... I am fine ...

The image of Miranda dying brought sadness to her eyes. Tears ran down her pale face, making Jonathan and Beatrice even more worried about her.

—Miranda is dead! My dear Miranda is dead, said Felicity.

More tears ran down her face. Felicity hugged Beatrice, who held her tight.

Jonathan stood up and went to the kitchen to fetch a glass of water.

—Drink, Miss Brown, he said when he returned. It will make you feel better.

Felicity left Beatrice's arms and faced her and Jonathan with a look of embarrassment.

—You will hate me after I have said what I am going to say now.

She took a deep breath before carrying on.

—I am not Miss Brown. I've lied to you all this time.

Jonathan and Beatrice looked at one another.

—That was an identity my friend Miranda created so you would accept our presence in your home. My name is Felicity, Felicity Worley.

Felicity saw the expressions of shock on their faces when she mentioned the name Worley.

—And I am married to Peter Worley, Felicity added.

Beatrice and Jonathan were speechless for a moment. Eventually Beatrice broke the silence.

—Why did you lie to us?

—My life has been a living hell for a long time. I was forced to marry him and have been suffering ever since we got married. He was never my choice of husband. My father forced me. I always heard great things about your beautiful work with the orphans and always wanted to come and visit your home, but I've never had permission to leave the house without my husband.

Felicity dried the tears that were falling down her face before carrying on.

—One day when my husband – I mean, Peter – one day when Peter ran away from town after he had murdered a man, Miranda helped me to have the courage to leave the house and knock on your door.

—Calm down, my dear, said Beatrice getting hold of Felicity's hands. You are shaking. Before you say any more, I want you to know that we love you and we understand why you felt the necessity to hide your true identity. Please stop pressuring yourself with this matter.

Beatrice looked at her son.

—We do understand your situation, she said. Don't we, son?

Still unable to speak from shock, Jonathan nodded. Felicity hugged Beatrice, feeling relieved. Jonathan remained immobile and looked pensive.

—The time I have spent here with you and the children, said Felicity, has been the only time in my entire life when I have felt happy and in peace, and although I have loved your company since the first afternoon I visited you, I never had the courage to tell you about who I really was. I was too scared that you would reject me and I would lose the only happy moments of my life.

—Forget about what happened, Beatrice assured her. Tell us –

what happened last night? How did you end up here and with blood all over your dress?

Felicity then told them everything that had happened the night before. Very emotional, she cried when she spoke about Miranda. When she finished, Jonathan held her hands.

—You're safe now, he said. We are going to look after you and this will be your home from now on.

Felicity looked straight into his eyes and smiled at him, looking more relieved after hearing what he had just said.

—That's right, Miss Brown …

Beatrice smiled at Felicity, realising her error.

—I mean, Felicity. Now, my dear, follow me. I'll take you to your room. You feel free to have a rest while I prepare you a lovely bath and find a new dress for you and also get some breakfast ready, as I believe you must be starving.

—Mother, said Jonathan, you look after Felicity and I'll investigate a way to help those children. That man can't just let them die.

—Please don't go, said Felicity. You're not welcome at the factory after all of those protests you arranged to stop the textile factory mistreating children. Peter is violent and I don't want you to get hurt.

—Don't worry, Felicity. After what you told me about last night I have a suspicion that Peter won't be around.

He kissed his mother on her forehead before leaving and told her he wouldn't be long.

—Don't worry, my dear, Beatrice assured Felicity. He will be fine. Knowing my son the way I do, there is no way he could have been at peace if he had not done anything to try and help those poor children. Let's pray that everything goes well.

Beatrice and Felicity went to the second floor where Beatrice showed Felicity to her room.

Felicity received new clothes brought by Beatrice and took a rest for the day. Beatrice looked after her throughout the day, making sure she was recovering well.

Hours later ...

—I am worried about Jonathan, said Felicity. It's past eight o'clock and we still don't have any news.

—I have asked for two friends of ours to go and look for him, Beatrice told her. I haven't felt any bad intuition, so I am sure my son is fine. Mothers can feel when something goes wrong. A mother's intuition never fails.

As soon as Beatrice finished her sentence the front door opened and Jonathan stormed in together with two friends. Jonathan and the other two men were each holding a child.

—We managed to get them out of that hell, said Jonathan.

—Take them to my room, suggested Beatrice. They can stay there until they recover.

Jonathan and the other two men went to the second floor followed by Beatrice and Felicity. They put the three sleeping children on a king-size bed, and once the two boys and the girl were comfortable, Jonathan covered them with a blanket.

—You did it! You rescued them, said Felicity looking happy and surprised.

—How are they? asked Beatrice.

—They are fine now. We took them to the hospital where I

153

could check them and give them medication but it was too risky to leave them there as ...

Jonathan looked at Felicity before continuing.

—It's your husband, Felicity. He is alive.

The look on Felicity's face changed to one of worry.

—I found out that Miranda had been left to die in your house, Jonathan continued, while your husband was taken to hospital by one of his men. He is at the hospital being treated.

—So he survived! exclaimed Felicity.

—Yes, he did. So when I heard the news I went to look for help. That was when Mr Robert arrived and told me that you had sent him to look for me, and together with Mr Sebastian we got help and went to the textile factory. All the staff were dispersing due to the news of Peter being at the hospital, so it was easy to get in and rescue the children. We took them to hospital where I gave them the initial treatment, but I thought I could help them here at home, which would also be less risky than staying at the same hospital as Peter.

—They look so ill, said Beatrice.

—They are fine now, mother. But they could have died.

Felicity didn't say a word. She was clearly upset about the news that Peter was still alive as it represented a threat to her. Jonathan hugged her when she started to cry.

—I know that you're scared now, he said, but I promise you that my mother and I will do everything we can to protect you. I asked one of the doctors about Peter's situation and he said that he is at risk, and the next twenty-four hours will be decisive.

The vision went blurry and slowly faded away. Michael had tears in his eyes.

—I know it's tough Michael, said Harriet.

They held hands and remained in silence until Michael broke down in tears.

—I remember now ... I was Peter Worley! I was the one who ... Michael couldn't finish his sentence.

Harriet nodded and continued.

—It was you who killed Jonathan and Felicity. They were both killed a few days after you left hospital by you and your crime fellows. I remained sad and lonely at the orphanage. Those were difficult times, as I had lost my son and I had to rediscover my faith in order to continue my life without becoming bitter and without letting the anger take over my soul. Jonathan was my only family. He was my treasure and his premature departure was a challenge to my faith. It's a terrible feeling for any mother to lose their son, especially at such a young age. I had to be so strong and believe that one day I would see him again. That was a test for my faith and I confess it was very difficult not to succumb. Years went by, and even though it was the hardest thing for me to do I managed to continue to run the orphanage until my last days. When I fell victim to a fatal illness, Mateo, Felicity and Jonathan were waiting for me. All that suffering I went through paid off when I saw them again.

—Beatrice, please forgive me, begged Michael. I am so ashamed of my actions ...

—Please don't call me Beatrice. I have taken you as a son, a son I want to inspire and help to see more and more the beautiful things of the divine truth. This is past now. You know I have forgiven you. We all did. Once we all reunited again we went to look for you and we found you living a very poor and miserable life. You had lost all of your money and properties to one of your crime fellows, who betrayed you and took

155

everything you owned. By the end of your days in that existence you were surrounded by lots of dark and inferior disincarnated spirits who wanted to cause you pain. Those spirits had been killed by you or your father previously, and when they found you they started to torment you with dark energy. They wanted revenge, and with that in mind they were stalking and tormenting you day after day. Because your energy was very low, your spirit allowed their energy to affect you. They drove you to alcohol addiction. You ended up dying of typhoid. It was a very sad passage. Very lonely and sad indeed. As we knew those spirits were hungry for revenge, we asked for permission from our superiors to collect you upon your passage and bring you directly to the Towers. Once here you were treated and attended the same school I now teach at so you could learn about your acts and learn how to work your spirit towards a purified existence. Jonathan and Felicity forgave you, as did Miranda. We all did, Michael. Although the reason why we incarnate to a new life experience is to evolve and purify our spirits through these obstacles, some spirits fail in their task, and you failed in your task in that particular experience. We all offered to incarnate again in order to help you and support your progress. Mateo and I incarnated first as your parents. Later Felicity incarnated as Gina, and Jonathan incarnated as your cousin Paul. Mateo had a very short time to live on the earth as he was needed on his missions back here, so he returned to the spiritual world when you were just a little boy.

—There's no need to feel ashamed, Michael, said Mateo. You went back for a new life test and loved your wife. You treated her well and with respect. You were an exemplary husband and father. You both did a good job in raising the children. You evolved. You are not that spirit who had to imprison others in order to have power. You learnt in your latest experience what you challenged yourself to learn when you were at the Towers: you learnt that you should love and respect the ones around you and never imprison anyone.

—You mentioned that Miranda has also forgiven me for what I have done. Where is she? I would like to talk to her ... to apologise to her.

—You have just spent months next to her, Harriet replied. Miranda has reincarnated as Gabrielle. She offered to incarnate as the daughter of a primitive spirit friend of hers who has been trying to progress but who unfortunately has been finding it very difficult to get rid of her vices.

—Nina, said Jonathan looking amused.

—Yes, Nina. Nina has been trying hard to leave her vices behind. Not just the drugs and the alcohol, but the vice of negativity. She has been delaying her progress by letting negative thoughts and depressive thoughts take over her soul. Every time Nina loses the faith, negative thoughts take over, and that's when she gets herself involved with drugs and alcohol. When this happens she attracts spirits with the same level of vibration, who only drag her further down. Miranda, as a more purified and elevated spirit, is there now as her daughter to give her the strength and support to succeed.

—What about Oscar?

—Oscar has had the same opportunity as Nina, which is to incarnate for another life experience and have a new chance, a new start. As you could see, unfortunately he failed once again. He spent his whole life nurturing bad thoughts. Always involved with inferior spirits, he delayed his progression and wasted another opportunity to elevate and purify his spirit. In a previous life he killed a man who ended up joining the legion. His negative and dark thoughts made him and his soul vulnerable to the influence of the legion, and you know what happened then.

—But why could God not save him from that horrible death – I mean, from that horrible passage?

—Because Oscar had chosen his destiny himself. We all have free will, don't forget, and therefore we all suffer the consequences, both positive and negative, of our own actions. God gave him the chance of a new start, a new life, and he wasted it completely. Had he become a good husband and a good father, worked hard for a living as a decent man should do, inferior spirits would never have been able to get close to him, because his energy vibration would have got higher and purer. Lowering his energy vibration allowed the legion and any other inferior spirits to get closer to him. The purer our spirits become, the closer to God we get.

—Help will come for Oscar or any other inferior spirit whenever they are ready to accept their mistakes and commit to change. Suffering is how spirits who are not elevated experience what is necessary for them to progress – as we have just seen with Felicity, for example. You could think that her experience was unending suffering, when actually that experience was an important learning experience for her, to understand what it's like to be imprisoned by someone else. What it's like to be controlled by someone else. She went through the same pain she had previously inflicted on others. Now Felicity, or Gina, has learnt never to control or enslave anyone. She learnt how to truly love.

Michael reflected on this for a few moments.

—What an amazing coincidence that Gabrielle and Nina now live in the same house where I used to live with Felicity over a century ago, he said.

—It's time for you to learn that coincidence doesn't exist, Michael. The universe always works in harmony and everything that

158

happens in life serves a purpose. It seems like you and Miranda, now Gabrielle, had to meet again. You looked after her with care and love, and perhaps that was part of God's plan – for you to return to earth, as you did before, when you ended up being arrested by the dark legion in the same house where she now lives incarnated. Remember when you asked how God could allow inferior spirits to behave in such a way? Well, what spirits like Buziba, Enu and so many other dark spirits don't know is that when they are acting they are still serving God's will. For example, they were key players in bringing you next to Gabrielle, Nina and Oscar, so you could redeem yourself with Gabrielle and have that experience. What they judged to be their way of punishing you was actually God's will to get you close to Gabrielle.

Michael was once again speechless. He was filled with one of the most honourable feelings: gratitude. Emotional, he held Harriet's and Mateo's hands.

—Thanks to you both. Thanks for helping me all this time. You have done so much for me by taking your time to advise me and guide my soul ... I also remember now that I have been so unfair on Paul. Things are very clear in my mind now. I can clearly remember that I was arguing with him. Paul was trying to calm me down and I lost my balance and fell down the stairs. He didn't push me.

—We know, said Harriet. We were there, don't forget. Before, you were so angry that your own anger was blinding you and hiding the truth, but the truth never dies, Michael.

—I also remember that before Gina, myself and Paul reincarnated I proposed having a short life so I could leave them to experience life as a couple and continue on their own towards their progression.

—That's right, son. They now have their individual tasks and

159

obstacles to overcome in order to continue their evolution. They also have the mission of guiding Harry.

—Yes, Harry. What about my son? Buziba mentioned him so many times and I recall him threatening Gina and Harry. Why Harry?

—Once Mateo returned to the spiritual world he came to find out that John Worley was at a spiritual recovery hospital located near the earth zone. He had been a prisoner of a group of inferior spirits, the same that wanted revenge on you and him. The legion. After many years suffering he finally asked for God's mercy and he was heard. Our friends rescued him and took him to a local hospital. After regretting all of his actions he requested a new chance, a new start. He then incarnated as your first son, Harry. He is now surrounded by love and has around him spirits who are dedicated to helping his progression.

—Kit and Grace?

—Correct. They are some enlightened spirits who have been mentoring him for centuries. As his progress has been very slow, the two spirits – in a very giving gesture – incarnated as his brother and sister so they can help and support him in his new experience. Right now they are limited, as they still have the limitations of a child's body, but soon, when they grow up and have fewer limitations, they will be more capable of supporting John, now Harry.

—Should we be concerned about Harry since the legion continues to chase him?

—Yes and no. We need to trust God and trust that Harry will follow the examples of love and respect that he has around him now, and therefore won't make the same mistakes as before. If that happens, the legion or any other inferior and dark spirit won't be able to approach him, as he will get closer and closer to God. But if, after all, he continues to delay his progress, then, yes, I am afraid he will be vulnerable to dark

160

energies.

Chapter XVII
The Assault

Six months later

Buziba was angry for revenge. John Worley had escaped once, and now he had found him incarnated he would not rest until he managed to bring him back to the spiritual world, where he could enslave him. He had asked permission for his leader to work on the case. His plan was to murder Harry and get hold of his spirit as soon as he underwent the passage. Buziba spent months following a young guy named Zack, who was only eighteen. Zack, who lived with his mother and father in a flat in Clapham, south London, had a perfect loving home, with two parents who always cared for and loved him. Suddenly, after a break-up with his girlfriend, he began to cultivate negative and depressive thoughts, lowering his energetic vibration, which was what Buziba needed in order to have access to him and act on his mind. Buziba followed the young guy for several months, sending him destructive and addictive thoughts on a regular basis. Day after day Buziba took advantage of the fact that the lad was getting more and more depressed and kept on sending him addictive thoughts, until Zack got himself completely addicted to heavy drugs. Family life became a hell, with both parents trying everything they could to help and get Zack away from the new druggie people their son started to get himself involved with, but nothing seemed to help. Zack had got completely involved with that world. His behaviour changed. He became aggressive and was no longer the bright and loving kid he had always been. He stopped looking after his hygiene, and a very low and dark energy could be felt on him. Zack ended up by leaving home and moving into a crack house where he was surrounded by others who had the same energy. He became increasingly influenced by inferior spirits who were feeding off the same addiction as him.

Today is the day he will pay back everything he has done to me and my family, thought Buziba, whose eyes were red with anger. *I will bring him back here and he will feel again how it feels to be a slave, how it feels to have his soul torn apart.*

He was no longer able to act on Harry's mind, as the boy was being heavily protected by superior spirits who worked at the spiritual home which Gina, Paul and the kids were frequenting on a weekly basis. He had learnt that Gina, Paul and the kids had gone Christmas shopping in London's West End, and Buziba had a plan to take advantage of Zack's vulnerability and use him to attack the family and have Harry killed. That way he could bring Harry's spirit back to the spiritual world and take revenge on him. The plan was to drive Zack to assault the family, leading to Harry's murder.

Gina, Paul and the kids were on their way home from a whole day's shopping in the West End. The kids were all tired from a long day of walking. Gina had Kit in the buggy whilst Paul was carrying Grace, who was asleep in his arms, and Harry walked between Gina and Paul.

—Maybe it wasn't a great idea to use public transport. The kids are all tired of walking, said Paul to Gina.

—You're right, but we are nearly home, honey.

—Mum, I am tired and hungry, said Harry.

—We are nearly home, dear, she assured him.

—Hey you! Give me your wallet!

The family was set upon by Zack, who was holding a gun.

Buziba had inspired Zack to wait in a deserted street near Gina's home knowing that Gina, Paul and the kids were going to pass by. Alongside five other dark spirits, Buziba kept on telling Zack to shoot Harry.

—Give me your wallet or I will shoot!

Everybody started panicking. Gina was shaking. Kit and Grace woke up and, able to sense the bad energy, they began to cry and scream. Noticing that Zack was visibly under the effects of drugs, Paul tried to calm him down.

—Calm down, boy. Please tell me, what do you want? Is it the wallet? That's fine ... We will give you everything you want, but please put the gun down.

—He is lying to you, Buziba said into Zack's ear. Just shoot! Shoot the boy! Shoot!

Harriet, Mateo and Michael were present, holding hands and praying. They had been advised that the family was going to need their support. Knowing that it wasn't a situation they were going to be able to interfere in, they were silently sending positive vibrations to Gina, Paul and the kids.

—Please leave my family alone, begged Paul. We are keen to cooperate with whatever you want.

—Go on and shoot the boy, Buziba continued to order. Shoot the whole family if necessary.

Michael got closer to Zack and Buziba and, using a very calm tone of voice, he spoke to Zack.

—This isn't you, Zack. You would never hurt anyone. Put the gun down. God is watching over you and wants you to know that he loves you. Think of your mother and father. Think of the moments you felt

164

secure and looked after when you were with your parents. They miss you and they want you back ...

The positive vibrations began to have an effect on Zack, who, inspired by the caring words of Michael, put the gun down.

—Good, Zack. Your mother cries herself to sleep every night thinking of you, wondering how you are. They love you so much.

Michael put his hands on Zack's chest and, focusing on his parents, sent him an immense amount of loving energy.

—Feel the love of your parents, he said.

Suddenly sirens from police cars could be heard. Paul put his hand into his pocket to reach out for his wallet, which made Zack panic. He picked up the gun and pulled the trigger, shooting twice.

—Yes, cried Buziba with joy. Well done, boy.

The whole family screamed. Harry and Gina fell back on to the floor. There was a pool of blood on the ground. Still holding Grace in his arms, Paul kneeled down, trying to reach out to Gina and Harry.

Zack ran, trying to escape, but was caught by three policemen who wrestled him to the floor and arrested him.

A guy in the street approached Paul.

—I saw that druggie approach you and called the police.

The same guy suddenly noticed the bleeding and realised the severity of the situation.

—Call an ambulance, please! shouted Paul.

Paul cried desperately over Harry and Gina, who were lying on the ground, bleeding.

Chapter XVIII
Gina and Michael Reunite

Gina woke up in a hospital bed at a spiritual colony near the borders with the earth and saw Michael sitting next to the bed watching her.

—Michael? Oh my God, is that you?

Gina shed tears when she saw Michael. She leaned forward and sat up on the edge of the bed.

—Oh my darling, how nice it is to see you.

They hugged each other very tightly and remained like that until Gina broke the silence.

—Michael, you passed away ... What am I doing here? Have I ...

—No darling, you haven't. You haven't returned yet. You were shot by a guy in an assault. Your soul has been treated at this hospital whilst your corporeal body is undergoing medical procedures at a hospital on earth.

Remembering what had happened, Gina put both hands on her face.

—Harry! she said. Our Harry was shot too! How's our Harry?

—He is fine. The bullet only reached his shoulder and he is recovering well. Paul, Isabel and Juliana have been looking after him and after Kit and Grace, too. They are all fine. Paul has been great looking after them. He has also been next to you at the hospital as much as possible.

—Is this my time to return, then? Am I not going back there

anymore?

—No. It's not your time to return home. You will be going back to earth soon. Your soul has been resting at this spiritual hospital because your corporeal body suffered some major injuries. Your body has been in a coma for quite a while now. It's been two weeks since the incident and your human body is now ready to receive your soul again, which means you are ready to go back. But I requested to see you before you went back.

They both fell silent.

—About you and Paul, Michael said eventually.

—I am sorry, Michael. I never meant to get so involved with him. It happened naturally ... He has been there supporting me and the kids, and suddenly I realised I ...

—You realised you had fallen in love with him, said Michael with tears in his eyes.

Embarrassed, Gina could not look Michael in the eyes.

—Yes. I do love him.

—Please, darling, don't feel bad.

Michael touched her face and gently lifted her face.

—I am very happy for you two, he said.

—You are?

—Yes, I really am. The love I feel for you now is not an obsessive and possessive feeling, as it was before. I love you as I love the kids, as I love my mum, and as I love Paul ... I have learnt to love you free of obligations. I did imprison you with my love and by trying to imprison you I ended up by imprisoning myself. I spent a lot of time and effort trying to control you, and I also wasted a lot of energy by feeling jealous of you and controlling you. Time and energy I should have invested in working on my own improvements.

—I am confused, Michael. You never did those terrible things that you're saying. You were an amazing husband and a lovely father to our kids. I couldn't have asked for a better man.

Michael remembered that Gina had not recovered her spiritual memory.

—I did bad things to you in a past life ... but that is in the past now. I just wanted to say thanks to you for helping me to be a better man. Thanks for showing me what real love means. I will always be grateful for what you have done for me.

They hugged each other very tightly. Both had tears in their eyes. They looked at each other with tenderness and happiness in their eyes.

Michael dried the tears on her face.

—It's time for you to be happy, Felicity. Go back and continue to grow as this beautiful woman you have been.

He took a long breath and stroked her hair.

—Now it's time for you to go back, my darling. You have three beautiful kids who are waiting for mummy. Don't forget that I am truly happy for you and Paul. You two are meant to be together. Goodbye now.

Mateo came in and held Gina's hand. He took Gina back to the hospital, where Paul was waiting, sitting next to her bed.

Michael left the hospital, and Harriet was waiting for him outside.

—Well done, son. I am so proud of you! Look how far you have come. Look back and praise yourself for how much you have achieved so far!

—Is she going to remember this once she is back?

—I am afraid not. She will have a vague remembrance, as if she had a dream, though I can assure you that her spirit will know you, and that's what matters.

Michael smiled.

—I feel free now, he said. I feel free from all the anger and rancour I was carrying with me, and – wow – it's a very good feeling.

He took a long breath.

—I'm ready to carry on now, he said.

Harriet and Michael held hands and walked across the field, heading back to the Towers.

Chapter XIX - Life Never Ceases

Two years later ...

Michael had spent the past two years studying and learning at the spiritual school. His spirit became lighter once he left the thoughts of possessiveness and obsession behind. Michael dedicated his time to accompanying and assisting Regina on her mission of inspiring Gabrielle and Nina to continue with their objectives. Nina, with the help of her daughter and spiritual friends, stopped drinking and slowly worked on getting her self-confidence back. She got a job and was making great progress. Gabrielle was a joy for all of those around her. At school she was the teacher's favourite pupil and the best friend to many of her classmates. At home Gabrielle continued to help Nina with the housework and was always caring and supportive. Their house had become a home, with love and care all around. Michael and Regina had paid daily visits to both of them to ensure their home was surrounded by energy of love and prosperity. Whenever they felt like there was any chance of Nina slipping back into her old behaviour they would send her encouraging thoughts and loving vibrations which helped to inspire her to continue her journey. With time the need for Regina and Michael to do healing sessions diminished as Nina evolved her spirit. Love is a very potent energy, and once Nina started to feed her soul with it she managed to change her entire life.

After ensuring that both mother and daughter were doing well, Michael took the important decision to reincarnate and put his spirit through a new experience. It was his time to put into practice everything he had learnt.

His last days at the Towers were difficult, as no spirit enjoys the idea of incarnating and being imprisoned in a physical body, with all the restrictions that the spirit has to suffer when living within a corporeal body. We all face incarnation like an exam that we aim to pass, and just as though he were revising for a big exam, Michael had a period of reclusiveness during which he needed to be silent and focus on all the obstacles he knew he would go through on his next incarnation. He took time to meditate, review the past and learn from his past mistakes to ensure a different future.

Months of reclusiveness went by, and on the day before his departure for a new start, Harriet and Mateo came in to give him motivation and encouragement and to say their goodbyes.

—I must confess I feel very apprehensive and a bit scared. But I am confident in my decision ...

—You will succeed, Michael, said Mateo. Be confident and be strong. You have come a long way and improved so much. Trust in the divine protection son. Incarnation is always a new chance to make it right. And this is a gift that our creator presents us with. Remember that you will have your spiritual friends visiting you to guide and inspire you to give you the motivation and strength to carry on.

—I cannot forget to thank you both, said Michael with a tear falling down his face. You have always inspired me and you have always believed I could make it.

—No need to thank us, said Harriet who also had tears in her eyes. You did it all yourself. We could advise you, we could give you love and show you the way, but it was down to you to make it happen and you are doing so well! We are very proud of you for everything you have achieved.

Months later ...

It was a mild and lovely spring day in London. The sky was blue with no clouds. The church bells were announcing the celebration of another wedding.

The crowd went outside the church, excited to see the new married couple leave the church. Isabel and new husband Francois left the church to find a rain of confetti being thrown at them by the guests.

Gina, Paul and the kids were among the happy guests congratulating the new couple. Grace and Kit were running around with other kids, Gina was holding hands with Paul, and next to them Harry was minding his new baby brother, who had been born only a few weeks before.

Harriet and Mateo arrived at that point to pay a visit to the family. Harriet shed a tear when she saw Harry holding his little brother. She put her hands above the two of them and prayed.

—Why are you crying? asked Mateo.

—Because I am happy. Take a look at them now.

Isabel and Francois got into the car that was waiting to take them to the wedding reception. Gina and Paul went up to Harry, who was still holding the baby. Grace and Kit came closer, gave Paul and Gina

172

a big hug, and then left to run around with the other kids again. There was an immense energy of joy and happiness all around.

Harriet turned to Mateo.

—Felicity, Jonathan, John Worley and Peter are finally in harmony and happy, she said. I am so proud of them all. They have come a long way to get to this moment.

Mateo exchanged a joyful smile with Harriet.

—Yes, my dear, he said. It seems like they made it.

Harriet and Mateo held hands and, feeling contentment for the happiness of those they loved, and feeling peaceful with the reassurance that we all sooner or later evolve and accept love in our lives, they returned to the Towers.

The End

Author's note

The idea of writing The Truth Never Dies came from the desire to share with others the comfort I found with the Spiritism doctrine and its teachings about the afterlife.

I was only eight years old when my mother passed away and as it happens with everyone who has lost someone whom we deeply love, I went through a lot of suffering and pain. As everyone who has gone through this circumstances I also had to carry on my with life.

When I was a kid I remember to go to bed at night, switch off the lights so my father wouldn't see me and then when I knew no one was watching I would cry and beg for my mum to come back. I grew up pretending I was strong and pretending I could face it but deep down I was still that little boy waiting for mum to come back home. It was later in life that sorrow and sadness took over and I had to decide to go in search of the answers.

Well, I found my strength and found my answers by deeply believing that our lives are infinite and that we are on a continuous evolutionary process. I still miss my mother as I do miss all the others whom I love and have passed away though the pain isn't there anymore because I learnt that we don't die. We only continue to progress. The separation is only temporary and I am sure of it.

I confess it would be almost impossible for me to have continued with my life, being so positive, if it wasn't for the assurance and certainty that we will all reunite again with those we dearly love and have already passed away.

I hope this novel has served its purpose of comforting all of those who have been broken heart. Try and imagine death as the freedom of our spirits towards the way back home.

Much Care

Valter Dos Santos

More information about the author;

www.superne-santos.blogspot.com
www.facebook.com/thetruthneverdiesbook
Twitter; @superne

Artcover by; Megan Corbally

Megan Corbally is an eighteen year old college student residing in beautiful North Carolina in the United States of America.
Specializing in abstract painting, drawing, photography, and writing, she has been practicing various forms of visual art for the majority of her lifetime thus far.
By the artist; *The painting used for the cover, entitled "Who Am I?",attempts to embody the basic idea that things are not always what they seem. People are, at their core, essentially all the same, but they see aspects of their lives from varying viewpoints and perspectives. This creates the beautiful illusion that we call life; if everyone saw ideas from the same angle, how would we be able to learn and grow from each other?*

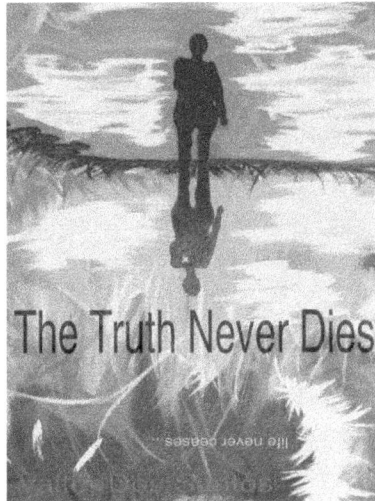

Depicted is a figure pondering the question the title asks. Does this figure see themselves differently than others see it? Can anyone accurately and completely answer this question?

"Who Am I?", 24in x 30in, acrylic on canvas, July 2010, Megan Corbally
To know more about Megan Corbally's work visit;
http://megbert.deviantart.com
For artist inquires email Megan at mlcorbal@ncsu.edu

Bibliography

The Gospel according to the spiritism, Allan Kardec

The spirits book, Allan Kardec

Extracts taken from; The Gospel according to the Spiritism, by Allan Kardec and The Spirits Book, by Allan Kardec, are of public domain

This romance is entirely a work of fiction. The names, characters and incidents portrayed in it are the work of the author's imagination. Any resemblance to actual persons, living or dead, events or localities is entirely coincidental.